Memories of a German Geordie

Seventy years of highlights and lowlights

C G Clemmetsen

Highlights

Lowlights

Lined up they guide ships into the Tyne

ISBN: -10-1463556144
ISBN-13:-978-1463556143

TO MY GRANDCHILDREN

Matthew, Louisa, Isak and Anna

Contents

ACKNOWLEDGMENTS

With grateful thanks for giving me inspiration
and encouragement to Ruth and Diane

Before my time

Father's parents   Mother's parents

A lifelong interest for me has been the desire to get to know people in other areas and situations and to travel, in order to see different landscapes and visit interesting or historical places. This may in part be explained by events before I was born. My mother's father had gone to Richmond/Virginia for some time to gain experience in the tobacco trade. Although he would have liked to settle there permanently, his bride-to-be (my grandmother) would not leave Germany. The only relic from his stay there is a rocking chair which I still treasure.

 My mother (Mutti) was born 1898. She had been a keen walker in her younger years and often described some of her adventures. Due to the war major travel plans were impossible, but every year, when the new railway timetable came out, Mutti went to get it at the central station and together we would be planning trips we were never able to make.

My father (Vati) was born 1879 and must have been a very independent little boy. Aged about twelve, he started from his hometown Husum, walking eastwards and kept on walking until he reached the town of Schleswig, about thirty miles away. On the way home he managed to get the odd lift on a farm cart. Two of his brothers had emigrated to South Africa and they persuaded Vati to join them there. They lived in a small town called Reddersburg, on the central plateau. The elevation caused Vati to develop asthma and he decided to return to Germany. Adventure-lust made him travel to Port Elizabeth, catch a ship through the Suez Canal and disembark in Alexandria. From there he crossed by boat to the southern tip of Italy and walked all the way home to northern Germany. Because he had enjoyed this so much, he retraced most of that journey with a friend a few years later. A special treat in my younger years would be a lie-in on a Sunday morning when Vati told me made-up travel tales, some based on places he had visited, others he only knew from books.

Also of note is that my father had been married to Helene Simon who died of cancer in 1929. Sadly, daughter Beate also died in 1935. Son Hans, born 1907, was farming in Friedrichstadt/Eider by then. Helene was Jewish and her brother Wilhelm with his wife Gerty saw how things were changing in Germany and decided in 1933 to emigrate to London with their twelve-year old son Bernard.

Vati was working in Lahr (Black Forest) adapting First World War barracks for use as a cigarette factory. The company was Reemtsma and Mutti's father worked for them after having given up his own little cigar factory in Herzberg/Harz. At my grandparents' house my mother and father met and discovered their mutual love of walking – of course they had the wonderful landscape of the Black Forest on the doorstep.

Mutti 30 and 70

1938 – 1945 War years

Volksdorf

At the time of my birth in 1938 my parents lived in a flat in the city of Hamburg. Vati was fifty nine and still working as an architect for a housing company in Altona. Everyone seems to have sensed danger and my parents decided to buy a house on the outskirts of Hamburg (Ahrensburger Weg 106 in Volksdorf). This proved to be the salvation for our little family as their previous home was totally destroyed, whereas we only suffered broken windows. Due to his age, Vati was not called up, but had to travel every day right across the city to check on the housing company flats. When the U-Bahn (local train) stopped running he went on his bike, cycling the 20 km there and back and I remember him returning late in the evening, black as a miner and completely exhausted after crossing the bombed parts of the inner city.

Mother's little helper

Most of our windows had been shattered by the blast from an incendiary bomb. Little though I was, I wanted to help Mutti and proceeded to clear the broken glass from the window sills with my bare hands. Needless to say I cut myself in the process and was left with a rather odd looking right middle finger. I might as well mention here how I managed to shorten the tip of my left middle finger as well a few years later. The finger had become infected, was swollen and so painful that I was taken to the doctor. We were told to come back when it was yellow, ready for lancing. For two or three days I was in great pain, but although the finger discoloured in various ways, it never turned yellow. At last Mutti could stand it no longer, took me back to the doctor who was horrified – we had left it far too long and were sent straight off to the hospital. There was talk of amputation and how little could they get away with in such a young child. In the end the doctor decided to remove only a bit of bone from the finger tip and try the new medicine that had helped many soldiers to survive – penicillin. It worked, but the same injury a few years earlier would have had far more serious consequences. I kept the tiny piece of bone for many years, it was riddled with holes, like a sieve.

Although our house had central heating installed, we had no fuel to run it during the war years and heated the living room with a stove. On top of this were always one or two pans with hot water. One afternoon I was on my own in the room, when one of these pans started to boil over. I knew that it was high time to move it more to the side, but I was too small and not really strong enough. I pulled, the pan jerked and boiling water sloshed down my right leg, scalding it from top to bottom. These burn wounds took many weeks to heal and I have terrible memories of the district nurse coming to change the tar dressing. I don't know what was more painful – peeling off the old dressing or applying the warm tar to the open wounds.

Bombs on Hamburg

In the outskirts we saw squadrons of planes flying over and witnessed incendiary bombs cause damage to houses and certainly to windows on a regular basis, but as a little girl of three or four I cannot remember really being frightened. Vati had made bunk beds which were in the basement, next to his workbench. German houses nearly always have a cellar of the same area as the ground floor. So we had the "Washing Room" which housed a huge copper boiler for boiling the laundry and the "Work Area", where Mutti's preserves were neatly stored on shelves Vati had made (IKEA did not exist in those days) and here space had been found for the bunk beds. The last room I can remember was the "Coal Cellar" where coal, peat briquettes and firewood were stored. The peat briquettes Vati made himself and I often watched him. First peat had to be cut into oblong shapes that were stacked up near the peat moors. When they were almost dried out, we went with a little hand cart, piled them high and pulled them home. They needed more drying before they could be used in the stove.

When the sirens sounded, whether it was day or night, we would leave the upper part of the house and go into the cellar. A very vivid memory is being carried by Vati, past preserves and Kilner jars on yet more shelves at the top of the cellar stairs, into the dimly lit and cool cellar rooms. Hamburg was most heavily bombed in the summer of 1943. It was a beautiful, warm summer that never seemed to end. I also remember standing with Vati on the back kitchen step and watch squadron after shining squadron fly over our house while Mutti was calling frantically from the cellar stairs for us to come down into relative safely. All I remember is the sight of the many silver planes in the blue sky – they were so pretty and I did not understand what it all meant.

On the most dramatic day, we got up in the morning, drew the blackout curtains back, only to discover that the blue sky had vanished and it was still dark even though it was getting up time. This must have been the worst of the bombing raids and the huge fires had resulted in a firestorm that had carried ash clouds as far as Volksdorf, about 12 km from the city centre. The garden was covered in burned paper fragments, ash and even books that were charred and had been wafted high into the air. During that day friends and acquaintances of my parents started to arrive. They had lost their homes, managed to come out to the suburbs and called on people they knew for shelter and help. I don't think either of my parents had spare time to take me on their lap and explain what was happening. Imagine, going to bed with 9 people, most of them strangers to me, bedded down wherever possible and finding 16 there the following morning. Most of them had rescued only a few possessions. I have no recollection how long they stayed in our house, but I do know that they all left eventually and it was some time later, before the period of 'lodgers' began. More of that later.

Evacuation

First of all: our Evacuation. The air raid warden called on everyone and told us that all women and children would have to leave immediately. We had to get to the train station in Ahrensburg. The train was immensely crowded and the heat was unbearable. The train travelled a while, then stopped and later continued without anyone really knowing where the journey would end. After many hours we arrived in Lübeck, normally about one hour by train from Hamburg. By this time it was early evening. Mutti was completely exhausted and decided that we should get off as she had a cousin in this town. I had not been to Tante Aenne's house before, but the cool, high rooms and the calm atmosphere left a lasting impression. As luck would have it, that night a doctor from Hamburg was visiting my aunt (she was a pharmacist). This lady was returning to Hamburg the following day and offered to take us back. Mutti was only too glad to accept. For me it is one of the little miracles of this time that we were never sent away again. The father of one of my friends did not hear from his wife and three children for months. They had ended up in Bavaria and did not come home until 1945.

Food

A little way along the road was a Flak Station and at night time we could see the searchlights, panning across the sky. As their barracks were right next to our little corner grocery shop we saw the soldiers regularly and started making friends with them. I think some of them must have been family men and missed their children. It was almost impossible to buy meat at this time and my parents had managed to obtain several rabbits. I had to go out every day to cut dandelion and other luscious leaves for them. Eventually the day would come for one of them to be made into a Sunday dinner. Neither Mutti nor Vati were able to cope with this chore. The answer came from the Flak station. We invited one or two of the men for lunch as long as they came the day before to dispatch the rabbit.

In large towns like Hamburg there was a great food shortage and at harvest time people from the town centre came to the suburbs for 'gleaning'. After farmers had harvested potatoes, word went round that on a given day at a certain time a field would be 'open'. Many people came by train and stood around patiently waiting for the farmers to depart. The waiting crowd then formed a line and began digging the field over again with small forks to find any potatoes left behind.

Just like in England, the government published hints to make the most of the little available food and use items that would not normally have been eaten. One example was bread made from maize (corn). It was quite yellow and tasted wonderful at first. However, unlike normal bread it had too much of its own taste and we did not really like it after a while. Many dishes needed a long time to cook or it was more convenient if the family was working in fields or gardens. Mothers then used a hay box where a hot stew could continue simmering for hours until the family came home.

My family was very fortunate in having a large garden as well as an allotment nearby where my father grew things like potatoes, turnips and onions. The garden by the house had many fruit trees, usually several varieties of each fruit: apples, three kinds of cherries, three kinds of plums, red, green and yellow gooseberries as well as all manner of vegetables: carrots, different beans, peas and asparagus. It meant we were never hungry, but it also left me with the memory of Vati on hands and knees, tending the young plants and Mutti occasionally in tears when she had to sit for hours, preparing fruit and vegetables for bottling, often late into the night. Having to shop for vegetables after getting married made me realise what a paradise I had been living in. The first year I was appalled for instance at the price for a small punnet of raspberries, thinking they would surely become cheaper. I waited and waited for the price to drop and eventually realised that the season was over. I was used to sitting in a cherry tree, picking and eating all I wanted, while reading a book at the same time!

Clothes

I cannot remember ever shopping for clothes as my mother made everything we needed. Occasionally, perhaps once a year, a 'home dressmaker' came to the house. She worked all day turning sheets, making dresses for me out of Mutti's old ones and generally turned her hand to anything one could make on a sewing machine. After the end of the war old German flags were available. The swastikas were removed and most girls had at least one red dress. Mutti learnt the technique of smocking in order to embellish the dresses a little. For my confirmation in 1953 I had the first dress made out of new material. It was navy blue and had a detachable white collar. This was my best dress for several years and came out for theatre visits and birthday parties. My second teenage dress was grey velvet, made out of an old dress Mutti had from before the war. Now I really felt grown up and sophisticated.

Primary School

School for me started in 1944. At that time the shortage of teachers meant, that we had a shift system, half the children went in the morning, the other half in the afternoon.

I was taken to school on the first day and when we emerged at midday, mothers were waiting to hand over the CONE. This is a German custom, where children are given a large colourful paper cone, filled with goodies – not too exciting in those days, compared to what they would contain now. From the second day onwards we walked to school by ourselves. This meant a twenty minute walk for me, but, of course, there was very little traffic in those days.

We were quite in awe of our teachers. At the beginning of class, everyone would rise and say 'Good morning'. I cannot remember that discipline was ever a problem. Naturally I would have been left-handed, but that was not permitted in those days and we were made to change to writing with the right hand. I believe that explains my untidy handwriting in some way, but it did have advantages, as I could write with my left when my right hand was injured.

Mutti also went to school one day a week. The purpose was not study, but to mend soldiers' uniforms. During these months friendships were formed which lasted for many years when the same women met on a regular basis, no longer for sewing, but just to get together over a cup of coffee and a piece of cake. I do remember Mutti coming home (this must have been 1945) telling Vati that she could not see the war lasting much longer because the uniforms and socks they had to mend were in such poor condition, often having been repaired previously.

As this was still a time of shortages, I remember having to go out into the countryside to collect acorns and beech kernels (to feed pigs) as well as blackberry leaves (no idea for what purpose). All these were handed in at school.

Mutti kept a wish list I had written out for Christmas – how would that appeal to a seven-year old in 2011?

A pair of wellington boots

More pocket money

Pale blue sport shorts

Adventure story book

A bowl of sweets and nuts

Frankfurters

Oranges

A trip to the Planetarium.

1945 – 1952 Growing up

May 1945

I remember the end of the war, - another warm and sunny day. We children were playing in the street (a dirt road at that time) when we heard a very strange sound in the distance. Adults came out and joined us at the roadside to witness what was happening. Can you imagine – a Scottish regiment in kilts came marching down the road to the accompaniment of bagpipes!

Lodgers

It must have been about this time that we first had permanent lodgers – people who had lost their homes in the inner city. At the beginning every room in the house was occupied by different families, but (like the 1943 visitors) they mostly left after some months as people made more permanent arrangements – perhaps with relatives in other areas. One man stayed with us for several years, he was a commercial traveller and very pleasant. Then the Timm family arrived. They had already lived in several other houses before they came to us. They had a boy, about ten and a girl, several years older. I could devote a whole chapter to events surrounding this family. Let it be sufficient to say that the teenage girl was sent out to befriend British soldiers who were stationed in a small hotel in the village. She came home with chocolates but more importantly British cigarettes which could then be traded by her parents on the black market for other things they wanted. These were very dark years for my parents as we could not persuade the Timms to look for a home of their own. They had never had it so good. I would say by 1950 nobody else in our area had lodgers anymore, but the Timms did not move out until 1953. I was then fifteen and their children, a few years older, had left home.

At last we had more space and we started to clean the rooms they had inhabited. The grime around the edges of the flooring was so ingrained, that it took us days on hands and knees to scrape it off with a kitchen knife. At last it was clean, we whitewashed the walls, put some of our furniture back and it was time for my first teenage birthday party. Mutti had 5 records: 3 Carusos, the Blue Danube and a carnival record. We borrowed a record player from neighbours and one or two of my friends also brought a few records along. Can you imagine, dancing to the strains of the Blue Danube for most of the evening!? You have no idea how smart and grown-up we felt.

Coupons

Just as in England, we had coupons and whenever a shop had a delivery of something, mothers and children went off to queue in the hope of getting at least some of it. Once our little group of friends found a few meat and bread coupons in the street. This would have caused great hardship to the family who lost them. To us it was the beginning of a day-long adventure. First of all each one of us went home to raid their piggy bank. We pooled our small change and set off to the village – a good half hour walk away. In the local Co-op we bought a small loaf of whitish bread, something we would not normally get at home. Now – what to do with the meat coupons. After long deliberations we decided we would get the best return by buying a sliced sausage made ¼ of meat, the remainder mostly of cereals; this was called "*Vierfache*". Armed with these goodies, the next decision we faced – where could we have our feast. Definitely not at home – we would be chastised for not having handed the coupons in. Another long walk, picking up a knife on the way, and we arrived at the local train station. There we made our sandwiches, cutting the bread on a counter that was no longer used. Why did we choose this odd location – I think it all just added to the general excitement of the day, even if it did mean giving a slice or two away to friends who were coming by to catch the train.

My room and books

By this time I had my own bedroom. It was quite small and narrow with a window overlooking the terrace at the back of the house. On warm summer nights I sat on the window sill and listened to the murmur of my parents' voices downstairs. Some evenings friends came over to play cards. These occasions were eagerly awaited by me as Vati was a good player and often won. The stake was 0.1 of a Pfennig, so winning or losing did not matter a great deal financially but to find 40 Pfennigs on the breakfast table next morning was wonderful for me.

One event haunted me for the next fifty years of my life. I had a wardrobe in my room and one night I must have been sleepwalking and had managed to squeeze myself between the wall and this wardrobe. I woke up, with my nose squashed into the back of the wardrobe, the room in darkness and I had no idea where I was. Many years later I could still wake up, terrified as I had dreamed that I was wedged between two boards, unable to escape. It was such a small event and yet remained with me for a very long time.

I loved reading and devoured the German equivalent to Enid Blyton: the Wild West tales, so vividly described by Karl May. This writer lived in Saxony and had never been to America, but Winnetou, Old Shatterhand and Old Surehand certainly were real for me. Perhaps a little later I discovered the Tales of 1001 Nights. This fascinated me to such an extent that I tried many ways of transforming my little bedroom into an Arabian tent with the aid of a large bedspread, rugs and cushions.

Girls' books never really interested me, but tales of foreign lands certainly did. My parents had some black and white books which I was allowed to get out on special occasions. There was a book on Rafael and several on the wonders of ancient Egypt. I loved reading travel accounts such as Thor Heyerdahl's 'Kon-Tiki' and books by the Swedish explorer Sven Hedin. I wrote to him and received a reply and a signed photo of himself which I have kept to this day.

At this time, aged perhaps twelve, a friend and I sometimes went to the Central Station on a Sunday. We stood on the walkway across the platforms and gazed at the indicator boards, dreaming of far away places when trains like the Copenhagen-Venice express came through. This really was a whiff of the big, wide world even though only a few of the carriages would make the whole journey and most passengers only travelled part of the route.

Holidays on the farm

After the war had ended I left Hamburg for the first time. Vati and I went to visit my half-brother Hans on his farm in Friedrichstadt. For me these were magical times, so different from life at home. There was my sister-in-law Traudchen and my two nephews Gerd and Hermann, four and two years older than me. There was also a refugee family from eastern Germany with a daughter, about our age. It was a mixed dairy and arable farm and the adults were busy all day long, having little time for us children. The boys already had a long list of duties, but we managed to play as well. Twice a day was milking time. Later they installed a milking machine, but at this time, we went with a horse and cart, laden with milk churns and milking stools to the meadow where the cows were grazing. I could only fetch and carry, but we had great fun, when the boys tried to squirt milk, fresh from the udder into each other's mouths. "Let's see, how far away you can stand!"

Haymaking was also fun. We were out all day, raking the newly mown grass over and making it into piles once it was dry enough. Traudchen came out at mid-day and brought a picnic lunch. It was during one of these wonderful summers that I suffered some accidents which had long-term consequences. On a particularly hot day Vati took me after lunch to the dyke by the river Eider. We lay on the sun-facing slope to have a siesta. Vati covered his head with a hankie, I pulled the apron from my dirndl dress over my face and then we fell asleep. It was obviously far too hot and later that afternoon I became very feverish and shivery. It turned out that I had suffered sunstroke. I was poorly for several days and confined to bed. A few days later I was feeling a bit better, was bored and decided that I would climb up into the hayloft to have a look at newborn kittens the other children had told me about. Halfway up the ladder to the hayloft, I felt dizzy, fell down and this time ended up with concussion. Mutti was not very pleased when we returned and I was not well enough to go to school at the beginning of term. This was the year we started learning Latin and I blame the delayed start of this new language for my poor grasp of Latin when other languages never seem to have been too much of a problem.

Toys and Games

Modern children have a great variety of different toys, and electronic games play an ever more important part in their lives. It was very different for us. The first toys I had (and have kept to this day) were made by my parents. One of the birch trees in our garden had been cut down and over a period of time Vati made all manner of items from this wood.

The first thing he carved was a tiny doll which was succeeded by a larger one with soft, moving arms and legs. I think Mutti must have carved the head, she certainly made the clothes for both of them. A year or so later, a wardrobe for dolls' clothes stood on the Christmas table and that year I made clothes for my little dolls out of every scrap of material I could find. A domino set, painstakingly painted by Mutti, was another addition, still from the same birch tree. Vati's most ambitious project was a pair of snowshoes (short skis) but despite his huge efforts of producing a smooth surface, they never really worked well. However, another family had a pair of proper skis and half a dozen kids took turns with this pair and my snowshoes. We all had sledges and enjoyed making snow eagles and igloos in the winter. When things got better most of us were given roller skates. The problem was that we had to walk quite a distance to a road that had a hard, smooth surface. – Another attraction in the summer was the open-air swimming pool, where we spent many happy hours.

The road where we lived carried very little traffic and it was quite safe for us to play ball games in the street. Sometimes the normal, easy way would become a bit 'boring' and we tried new games or other ideas. One of these was using half a brick instead of a ball. It was getting dusk and in the general excitement the brick-ball landed on my head. I can still see myself on the bathroom stool, peering through a curtain of blood-red hair while efforts were made to clean me up. Minor injuries were common as we often negotiated bramble thickets in order to build dens or we climbed trees. A popular 'dare' was to climb up one tree and then cross over onto the next one while perilously hanging, monkey-like, in the upper branches. "I bet you can't reach the end tree!!!"

Purzel

A favourite pastime for us was 'roaming' or '*strömern*'. We lived really on the very edge of Volksdorf where open fields, heath and wooded areas were not far away. One summer we

built a shelter out of dead branches, heather and soft, dry grass. Can you imagine our absolute amazement when we returned after a few days to find baby rabbits in our den?

For man years we had a dachshund called Purzel. He always came along and we managed to train him to look for us children when we were playing Hide and Seek. One child held Purzel until the others had hidden, then let him off and he would rush around until he had found most of us. After a while he gave up on this and started to go down the rabbit holes which were abundant in that area. He dug furiously to widen the hole, always to no avail, but when we came home at night his eyes were swollen and red from all the sand in them. Mutti had to sit for a long time and carefully remove this sand with the corner of a clean hankie.

Bicycles

I mentioned earlier – it was a good half an hour's walk to the village where most of the shops were. At the time of shortages this was particularly irksome because the shops frequently had already sold out by the time Mutti got there. We obviously needed a bicycle – an item at that time as rare and precious as a Mercedes car today. My parents had a pair of matching wardrobes in their bedroom and one of these was eventually traded in for a rather old bike. Soon after I had learnt to cycle, it became my job to go shopping in the village. At the beginning I was timid and careful, but after a while confidence grew and one day I could not resist going a different, longer way which involved cycling down a slope towards a footpath next to the railway line. It was exhilarating, dashing down the slope; there was just one problem – I did not know how to stop. The bike collided with the railway fence and when I picked myself up, I discovered to my great dismay, that the front wheel was so bent that I had to push the machine all the way home, much embarrassed by the loud squeak. Despite Vati's efforts with hammer and mallet, the front wheel was never really straight again! The wobbly front wheel was a permanent reminder and warning for me. As we got older, my friends and I went further and further a-field. Purzel's little legs could not keep up with the bicycles, so Vati fixed a wooden box to the rear carrier where he sat cheekily looking out - to the amusement of passers-by.

High School

At the age of twelve it was time to leave primary school and move on to the grammar school. The *Walddörfer Schule* had been designed by the renowned architect Fritz Schumacher and had been completed in 1931. On the site were buildings for the primary, secondary modern and grammar schools as well as a large sports area, shared hall and shared sports hall. It was possible to hold classes on the flat roof although this design feature was not used as much as had originally been planned, due to the frequently needed repairs after prolonged rain.

For the first few years our class teacher was Herr Bollhorn (Bolle for short) who was one of the teachers who helped to shape my personality. Walking straight, being independent and self-reliant were attributes he encouraged in us. A few anecdotes from the annual school trip may illustrate some of these facts. Our first trip, aged twelve, was to a small village, only about 20 miles from Volksdorf. We cycled there and accommodation was in a barn. The boys had to sleep on one side, the girls on the other. As a 'Thank You' to the farmer Bolle had volunteered our services to clear a pretty large field of weeds. As we toiled for several hours, rebellious feelings grew and by teatime we had decided to escape during the evening as an act of defiance. A few weeks before the trip we had read a poem called "The Dance of Death" and we wanted to enact this in the local cemetery. We had decided that only two children would get up at a time and the next two would have to count to twenty before they could get up, walk across the straw and out of the barn door. Imagine thirty children having to patiently wait their turn. By the time about half of the class had managed to get out, we suddenly realised that Bolle was standing in a shadowy corner, watching our silent procession. He could have easily told us off and sent us back inside, but instead he said how pleased he was to have us all out on such a fine night, ideal for a bit of stargazing. This completely took the wind out of our sails and by the time we finally were bedded down again, everyone was truly tired. However, this incident set the scene for every one of our future class trips – at least one escape had to be staged during the course of the week.

The following year we cycled again, but this time we moved on every other day, staying in Youth Hostels. Bolle divided us into groups of five or six, calculated how much money we would need per day for provisions and handed this sum to the groups every day. He left it to us how we wanted to spend the money. Some groups bought sensible items like bread, margarine, spreads and perhaps some fruit while others went wild and invested their new-found wealth in cakes and sweets. It did not take them many days before they realised the error of their ways. A boy in my group had discovered a shop that sold large tins of jam. We bought one of these with the intention to sell some of it off to the other groups, thus earning a few extra pennies for ourselves. Unfortunately the tin fell off the bicycle, the pop-on lid popped off and the jam started spilling out onto the pavement. Shock - horror at first, but it did not take us long to remedy the situation by scooping the jam back into the tin, hammer the lid down and later to sell the jam to our unsuspecting class mates.

Fun at School

Although we had to work quite hard, there were also many highlights. Every summer there was a huge sport competition, attended by many parents. There were races, athletics and gymnastic displays. In the winter different classes performed plays and there was always a summer and a winter ball. That was the official fun but we found more ways for entertainment. In the early summer large brown beetles appeared, mostly living in beech hedges (*Maikäfer* or May Beetles). In the morning these beetles were so cold and covered in dew that they could hardly move. We had prepared jam jars by piercing the lids in several places for beetle transport. On the walk to school we passed long beech hedges and vigorous shaking caused the beetles to drop to the ground, ready for collection. We filled a jar and placed it in a corner of the class room – lid removed. As the sun began to shine into the class room, the beetles warmed up and started to emerge. Soon the classroom was swarming with loudly buzzing insects.

Equally effective was the alarm-clock trick. Several children brought an alarm clock and they were then set to go off at intervals throughout the lesson. Most of our teachers coped very well with these pranks, although it must have been very annoying for them. Usually sanctions for the whole class followed, but we did not mind that at all.

Care Parcels

After the war had ended, just as here in England, it took a long time before the food situation improved. The first help we received was via Care Parcels. These were American ex-army rations which were distributed to the schools. These wondrous items were not always easy to share out and I remember Mutti shedding tears when I proudly arrived home with chewing gum and a packet of peanuts. The parents were happier when their child brought some flour or a lump of white cooking fat (similar to Trex here). This came in large 10lb tins as did the corned beef and was divided up by the teacher in charge.

Mutti had a friend who had emigrated to New York before the war. When American individuals were allowed to send their own parcels, they could obviously include things more suitable to a family's needs. For several years Mutti's friend sent us such a packet for Christmas and it's arrival was always eagerly awaited. In Germany it was not the custom to individually wrap presents, but everything was laid out attractively on the sideboard on Christmas Eve. I can still visualise packets of Sunmaid Raisins and Quaker Oats. The first year we only received food but the next time Mutti's friend had included a doll for me that could drink water and wet itself! Another year a Viewmaster and some discs gave us a first glimpse into the wider world. Remember, there was no TV and I could sit for ages looking at pictures of Manhattan, the Niagara Falls and the Grand Canyon.

The blockade of Berlin darkened the horizon again, but was relieved by the *Luftbrücke* when British and American planes flew in vital supplies and often took undernourished children back to the West for a holiday. Germany was no longer divided into four parts, but into the Russian zone and the three western zones where people were allowed to travel about. Now it was our turn to help. The school appealed to parents for assistance and we took things like tea, coffee, hand cream, soap and chocolates to send to distribution centres in East Germany. Remember, how much we had enjoyed the pretty American packages. The Russians did not allow anything printed into the country which meant that we had to scratch every bit of writing off the tins and obliterate any description from the boxes of food. Three of our class had volunteered to deal with these items – and what an adventurous day this was for us - we did this for several years. First of all we had to travel halfway across Hamburg to a de-fumigation centre. Not only the clothing but also all the other items had to be placed into a de-fumigation chamber for some time. When they had thus been made 'safe' we were at last able to make up the parcels. We had come prepared with gift wrap, brown paper and string. Then followed another journey to a Russian depot where we could leave these parcels. This adventure took about twice as long as the school day, but it filled us with a mixture of excitement and also dread of the regime in the East.

1953 – 1959 Teenager

Elmshorn

Life was getting much easier now. The Timm family had left and we had the house to ourselves again. In 1953 Vati fulfilled his pre-war promise and took Mutti to Venice. For me this was also to be a very special summer. My friend Christa Eschenbach (Esche for short) had persuaded my parents to allow me to attend riding lessons with her. We had been going most of the winter and had often helped mucking out and grooming the horses in return for extra lessons. This was good preparation for the six week course I attended in the Elmshorn Riding School. These were magic weeks for me, everything was so new. Sleeping in dormitories and eating canteen meals were quite an experience, but most important of all were the long and strenuous days in and around the stables. We had to help with all the tasks: grooming, mucking out, polishing the leather harnesses and shining the brasses. The highlights, of course, were the lessons. Most of these were dressage lessons in an arena, although occasionally we did some cross country work. We also learnt to drive a carriage and pair of horses and

I have a bronze medal to show, that once upon a time I was able to do this.

The experience was greatly enhanced by the fact that this was the home of the best German show jumper at that time (Fritz Tiedemann) and we were fortunate enough to be there when a show jumping event was held at the centre with big names from the national and international show jumping circuit competing.

Still in 1953 Tante Gerty and Onkel Wilhelm came over to Hamburg for the first time since having left in 1933. They stayed with us and invited me to visit them the following summer. At that time the Hamburg schools ran special trains for children who were going to spend some weeks in England. Most of the other children went to families who had volunteered to keep them, but were total strangers. I was lucky - at least I knew my host family.

However, it was a huge culture shock! My aunt was a truly remarkable person. She became an expert in anything she started. Before the war she had studied photography and ended up taking portraits of many famous people, politicians and film stars. While I stayed with them she was into painting and exhibited and sold her work. She was also a very good cook and – yes you have guessed it – she published a cook book. They were very kind to me, but hard taskmasters at the same time. I was not allowed to read any German books and I remember struggling one whole summer with 'Pride and Prejudice'. She also sent me off to shop for vegetables and groceries and questioned the shopkeepers on her next visit whether I had really asked for weird items like *onions or lettuce* by name or had only pointed them out.

by Onkel Wilhelm 1953   by Tante Gerty 1954

While I was with them the Horse of the Year Show took place in White City Stadium. I knew that Fritz Tiedemann and his grooms, who had become friends the previous year, would be there. My uncle had no interest in horses, but agreed to take me for the afternoon session. Whether it was the event itself or my enthusiasm, coupled with a visit to the stables and hobnobbing with the stable lads, I will never know, but we were carried away and also bought tickets for the evening events. Mobile phones had not yet been invented and Gerty was almost beside herself when we rolled in not long before midnight.

Pocket Money

When I was sixteen Vati thought it was time to teach me the value of money. Mutti and I had to draw up a list of the types of clothes and shoes I normally would need in a year. This was roughly costed and the result divided by twelve. He added the usual small amount of pocket money to this sum. When my friends heard about the astronomical amount of money I was given compared to them, they were quite envious. My euphoria did not last long though. I soon realised that I would have to save almost every penny for a month or so before I could buy a pair of shoes or larger item of clothing (there was no Primark in those days either). I was too proud to admit defeat and I know that this method caused me to be careful with money for the rest of my life. Later we repeated this experiment with Nils, but when we discovered that he used quite a bit of his pocket money to buy expensive bicycle parts, we wondered how he would get on. Again, the result was impressive. He often bought 3 pairs of old jeans in jumble sales, cut the worst pair up and used the good pieces to mend the other two pairs. He thereby became an expert with the sewing machine, made a tailored shirt and later even saddle bags for his cycling trips. A few years later brother Michael also tried his hand at tailoring. He used his skills to alter high quality men's suits he bought in second hand shops. Most of the previous owners had been rather portly and Michael was very slim indeed.

Monruzy

As I mentioned before, competitive sport was valued greatly at my school, but I was never very good at the 100m races. When I was seventeen, I felt it was time to improve my image. Perhaps I could manage better in a 1000m race? I must have tried too hard and ended up collapsed and with a slight heart condition. The doctors suggested that I should rest for a few months before returning to school. My condition improved sooner than expected and my parents now made a very momentous decision. They scraped together everything they could afford and sent me to a finishing school in Switzerland. They hoped that I would come out of my shell - being an only child I was extremely shy and tongue tied.

Going there really was a baptism of fire for me. Most of the other girls had arrived in September and were staying for a year. They had settled in and made friends by the time I arrived in January. I had to share a room with Sarah, a Dutch girl, who was also new, although there was a huge difference- a family friend of hers was already there. Sarah's father had lost most of his business due to the German invasion and you can imagine - there was still great hostility between Dutch and Germans in 1956. I cannot recall how long I suffered in silence when the three or four Dutch girls came into our room, settled themselves on her AND my bed, chattered away in Dutch, leaving me barely enough space to cower in the corner. Eventually the mouse spoke up which surprised them so much that from then on they spoke the regulation French and included me in their group. Sarah and I have stayed in touch ever since!

Monruzy was a small institution, run with an iron fist by Madame, her husband Monsieur and Mademoiselle Piaget. Their assessment described me as having *"sentiments profonds et harmonieux, trop timide, parfois un peu trop dans les nuages"*. Madame taught house keeping skills, Mademoiselle was responsible for food preparation and presentation and Monsieur taught French and Esperanto. The latter was voluntary but one of his hobbies. We were kept strictly on the premises, apart from Saturday afternoon outings to the town as long as we could all agree either to visit the cinema or go to a café. Mademoiselle had to go with us and not let us out of her sight. The virtual incarceration caused most of us to pile on the weight. How was that? -You may well ask. We were allowed to use as much bread and butter as we liked as well as sugar. I imagine Madame thought we would have a slice of bread and a spoonful of sugar in the tea. Instead we cut thick slices from the large loaves, smothered them with butter and poured the sugar on as thickly as possible before it slid off. From the Saturday outings we sometimes brought back jam or cheese. A few girls would plan A PARTY. One of us emptied a drawer and we filled this to the brim with sandwiches. After lights out we crept to the designated room, lit a few candles and devoured the enormous amount of sandwiches. I wonder how teenagers today would have coped with this lack of personal freedom!

Back in Hamburg

The method had obviously worked. When I returned to Hamburg I was brave enough to try things I would have never even contemplated before. I wanted to earn some money and thought my newly won French language skills might as well be put to some use. I wore my best summer dress and called on the top hotels in Hamburg, offering my services as a city guide for foreign visitors. I only got a few calls out of this, but for my parents it was proof that my confidence had grown enormously.

Bournemouth

By now I had decided not to return to school and study for the German equivalent of A-levels, but to work with languages. We felt that I needed to improve at least one other language in addition to French and my parents enrolled me in The Anglo Continental School of English in Bournemouth for three months from October to December 1956. I lived with the Rabbit family as a paying guest. My parents had given me some pocket money to spend, but I did not want to be more of a burden than necessary for them and determined to bring most of the money back. This made me extremely frugal. I was often hungry in the afternoons and bought the cheapest item bakeries had: crumpets. I chewed these leathery, dry things without any enjoyment at all and it was many years later when I was offered hot buttered crumpets for the first time that I realized how delicious they were when served properly.

One of our teachers was Mr. Crawford. He was Scottish but had been in business for many years in Canada, only to return to the UK after he retired. He soon got bored and applied to the language school for a teaching post. This was another teacher who influenced my life in important ways. Rather than joining the other tutors in the staff room, he gave up several lunchtime breaks each week to teach us bridge. Our little group comprised two Swiss men, Margrit Zwicky and Barbara Heibutzki. Margrit is Swiss, Barbara fled from Poland as a girl aged twelve and now lives near Bonn. Partly thanks to Mr. Crawford, we became such good friends that we have kept in pretty close touch to this day. He may not have had any formal training as a teacher, but he had some excellent ideas how to improve our English. He suggested for instance that we should buy a quality newspaper on Sundays. Furthermore he recommended that we should take just one article and study this carefully, looking up every single word we did not know. At first it seemed a waste of money to buy a whole paper and only read one article, but how would I otherwise have learnt the meaning of expressions such as *kith and kin* or *uncouth*?

For those who do not know: 1956 was the beginning of Rock'n Roll and I was at the right place to see it happen. One of the other students told us about a dance (the first of many). It was all a bit mysterious. We had to assemble at The Square in Bournemouth. They had hired a bus and off we set, into the dark night, not knowing where we were going. After a while we arrived at a barrier, guarded by armed soldiers, but were admitted. I think it must have been Hurn RAF station (now Bournemouth Airport, some 8 miles away). The dance was held in the canteen and we bopped around for hours to the sounds of Rock around the Clock. Now what do you drink if you are not used to this kind of outing and do not wish to spend much money. Some suggested Whisky and coke. I hated the Whisky and diluted it with the coke, making it last the whole evening. There was not much pleasure in this lukewarm concoction but these evenings were very exciting indeed.

Smog

In Bournemouth I experienced my first pea-souper or Smog (a combination of smoke and fog). Most people had open fires at that time. By mid-afternoon these were lit and gradually smoke started rising from the chimneys. On foggy days visibility became very poor and the acrid smell filled ones nostrils. - Barbara had invited me to visit her. I had not been to her house before, but knew roughly where she lived. When I came out of our house, I could hardly see the hand in front of my eyes, but carried on. At every turning I had to bend down and feel the road signs with my hands, trying to make out the street names. Luckily I did manage to find my way there and home again.

Television

I had never seen a TV in a private home, only in a shop-window. The Rabbit family had a tiny black and white set with a lamp perched on top – the room was in darkness and this light was supposed to make watching television less damaging for the eyes. The neighbours came round every night, 5 chairs were lined up, the lights turned off and the telly on. As far as I can remember there was only one channel which we watched in silence until 9 o'clock. Then Mrs. Rabbit made tea and the cups were passed from hand to hand without anyone ever taking their eyes of the TV! After a week or so of this, I started going out with my friends at night and Mrs. Rabbit asked uncomprehendingly 'but it is your favourite quiz show tonight!' One evening a week she went to her daughter who washed and set her hair. Occasionally I went with her. We studied the Radio Times and timed our walk home in such a way that we would only miss one programme. Then television had power over our lives due to its novelty, now it has power over our lives due to instant reporting, advertising and reality shows.

A nice cup of tea

The Rabbit family tried to make me welcome when I first arrived. 'What do you like to drink, dear – do you like tea?' I told them I only had one cup a week (this was true as my parents only had tea on Saturday afternoons). Mrs. Rabbit thought I did not know the difference between *week* and *day,* as she consumed about 12 cups of tea during the day, but eventually she realised that I did not drink much (far too little liquid intake, as I now know). My real tea ordeal came on Sunday mornings. There also was an Irish lodger and we were both served a cup of tea in bed as a special treat. Now to the bed! I was used to Eiderdowns from home and found the tightly tucked in sheets very uncomfortable to sleep in. Before climbing into bed I always pulled the sheets halfway out, to stop my toes being squashed. When I heard Mrs. Rabbits going down to make the tea on Sunday mornings, I got out of bed, into the freezing cold bedroom, tucked the sheet back in, so that she would not have a heart attack when she saw my 'untidy' bed. Back in bed, I thanked her for the tea which I absolutely hated. I had to wait till all was quiet again, then crept quickly along the passage to the bathroom, emptied the tea and returned to a now cold and uncomfortable bed. I obviously had not got over all my original shyness.

Rackow Schule

September came and I enrolled for a year's commercial course with English, French and Spanish at the *Rackow Schule*. Here I met Ingrid Flöter who has remained a friend to this day. One special event from that time was meeting Herrn Heinimann. Ingrid and another girl I had met at the school had not lived in Hamburg very long and at lunchtimes we sometimes explored different areas of the city. One such day we climbed the tower of *St. Michaelis Kirche* (Michel) near the harbour. While I was showing them the various sights from this high vantage point, an elderly gentleman asked whether he could join us. When it was time for us to go back to college, he explained that as a young man he had been an apprentice gardener in the vicinity and, now in his seventies, he had returned for the first time. It really would make his holiday special, if we would write to him sometime after his return. We exchanged addresses and then he asked us to choose a favourite song. We started on the long descent down the spiral staircase, giggling about this funny old man. By this time he had taken a recorder out of his breast pocket and played our chosen tunes; this echoed wonderfully in the huge tower. We soon stopped giggling and ended up quite touched by the experience.

Herr Heinimann

There is a sequel to this little event which I will insert here. Some weeks after the meeting a large yellow envelope arrived with a poem, several pages long, describing his encounter with three young maidens on top of the Michel. I replied to this and we corresponded regularly for the next three years. He often went on trips for gardeners and had a most poetic way of describing these days and the gardens they visited. In 1959 I told him that I was about to be married and he thought he could no longer write to me. Oscar, naturally, had no objections to this correspondence and so it continued. When Nils was born in 1961 he sent a £10 note and the same three years later for Michael. The letters became very infrequent and when Oscar and I had the chance to visit my Swiss friend Margrit (now married to Ernst) for a few days in 1968, I phoned Herrn Heinimann and we arranged an afternoon visit. He had prepared juice and cake for the 4 of us, but we had great difficulties finding anywhere to sit. He obviously lived the life of a recluse, had never thrown a newspaper out since his wife had died twenty years earlier, and filled the house with jams and preserves, in double rows all the way up the stairs. He made us most welcome and gave me the £10 note he had exchanged at the bank two years earlier when Thomas was born. He had not managed to send it, but kept it, just in case. My friend sent me the announcement of his death about a year later. This is not a momentous story, but shows how a small event often can have lasting effects.

Lloyd's Register of Shipping

I was determined to use at least one of my languages and was delighted when I found an advertisement for a job, actually written in English. I applied for the position of *Auslands Korrespondentin*, literally translated this means foreign correspondent. However, in German it only indicates a secretary who can use several languages. The choice was a good one – more than half of the Surveyors were British and English was the lingua franca at work. The office extended over two floors in a centrally located office block in Hamburg. Of course, one could climb the four floors by stairs, but the alternative was the Paternoster lift. These are considered to be dangerous nowadays and at first I was quite wary of it as well. Each little cabin was open and the cabins moved continually upwards in the right shaft, down in the left one. As the cabin approached you just stepped on board. The London Eye works on the same principle but is much slower. It took me quite a while before I was brave enough to travel the whole way round – logic told me that the cabin would remain the right way up at all times, but there was the sneaky fear, that this might not be so once the loft was reached!

We worked hard and conscientiously at all times and the following little incidents took place during our lunch time. The office windows looked out onto a narrow road at the back and straight opposite was a bakery. We used to buy their delicious cakes from time to time when one of the girls had a birthday. Rather than waste time and effort by going all the way down, we arranged with the shop that we would ring them, place an order and a short while later we lowered a basked with money all the four floors down and they put the cakes into it. We never found out what people in the offices below made of the descending basket!

Three of the Surveyors worked on plan approval and rarely went to the shipyards during the day. One of them was Oscar, my future husband. He was a keen Scottish Country dancer and offered to teach us girls some of these dances. One lunchtime a week we pushed the desks in the main office to the sides. Oscar brought his record player along and taught us various steps. This went on for a considerable time until one day the big boss arrived back sooner than usual from his lunch break, only to be greeted by music as he entered the lower office – the telephone girl who could not leave her position, had switched the intercom to 'receive'. You should have seen Mr. Walburn's face when he stormed upstairs, but to our amazement, he let us continue with the dancing lessons, only the telephone girl was no longer allowed to listen in downstairs to prevent visitors getting the wrong impression.

A romantic tale

Three of us worked in one small room. Whenever Oscar phoned, I could not really understand him because he spoke so fast and I would hastily hand the phone to one of the other girls. They had been there several years and were more fluent in English than I was. During the winter I had taken evening classes in English in order to sit for a higher examination from the Chamber of Commerce. By this time I had discovered that not one of the three Surveyors I typed for was a really reliable speller. I consulted my colleagues and was told that Oscar Clemmetsen could not only spell, but was also taking German lessons. Timidly I asked whether he would correct a few translations for me, prior to the impending examination. This he did, I passed and he took me out to dinner to celebrate. The rest, as they say, is history.

The autumn of 1959 was one of the golden ones - summer did not seem to want to end that year. We were engaged in September and married in November in Hamburg. We spent our honeymoon in Heidelberg and the Black Forest and were able to take long walks in sunshine every day. We had decided that we would not eat in the same place twice. There are many small breweries in this area and almost every Gaststätte (pub) served a different beer in rather attractively decorated glasses. One could buy these for DM 1 and consequently we arrived home with quite a stock of pretty beer glasses.

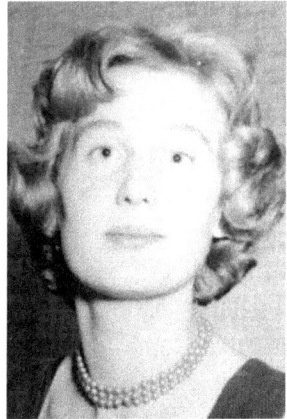
1960

1960 – 1971 London

Friern Barnet

Oscar had rented an upstairs flat in Friern Barnet, this was situated on a busy junction, above a Launderette. It needed quite a bit of decorating, a skill which was completely unknown to me. Needless to say I wanted to impress my new husband and started in the kitchen with great enthusiasm. Oscar was a kindly man and found words to let me know that the kitchen door would have to be rubbed down a second (and third) time and should not show rivulets of dried paint when finished. Oscar had learnt these techniques in his younger days when he had built several small boats. Well, the training stood me in good stead because by the time we started on our first house, I had become the door painting expert!

Having the launderette downstairs was very useful indeed. I could go downstairs, load up the washing machine, go back up to wash the breakfast dishes, and return just in time to take the clean washing out. I really was pretty clueless, but keen to do well. So what should a girl do with a grubby duster – yes, you guessed it, put it in the wash. That day all of Oscar's office shirts emerged cream coloured rather than sparkling white – not a pretty sight. I had also been told that clothes ought to be aired. Consequently I put suits and dresses on the balcony to air. I had a navy wool dress which I was rather fond of. When I looked for it one day, it had disappeared from my wardrobe. After I told a neighbour about my loss, she mentioned a navy jumper she had seen lying around the yard by the dustbins.

When I went to investigate I found my dress, shrunk to about half its former size. It must have blown down into the yard, got wet and dry again for days and days and certainly was no longer wearable. This event curbed my enthusiasm for airing clothes.

Oath of Allegiance

Anyone who marries a British citizen is entitled to apply for British nationality. Lloyd's Register recommended that we should do this for me just in case Oscar needed to be posted to a country where a German passport could create difficulties. The first few weeks after our wedding were occupied with decorating and Christmas preparations and the nationality problem had almost been forgotten. Shortly before Easter we decided to spend Easter in Paris. Suddenly the passport issue was urgent as I had not had my German one altered to the married name. Furthermore foreign nationals had to report twice a year in person to an office in central London. I had done this once and had sat around for hours – another reason for becoming a British citizen quickly. After obtaining the necessary forms I now had to find a solicitor in order to swear an Oath of Allegiance to the Queen. This caused me a great deal of anxiety – how loyal and devoted did I feel to Her Majesty? In the end common sense prevailed and I made an appointment with a local solicitor. I was suitably impressed with the Dickensian office – large piles of papers tied with pink ribbons were to be seen all over the floor, it looked very important. Soon I was shown into the solicitor's office. The gentleman was on the telephone, pointed to a chair near his desk and proceeded to leaf through my application papers while still talking into the phone. Again he waved and indicated that I should read the oath. A few moments later I was back in the outer office, paid the fee and felt completely disillusioned at the casual way he had treated this event which felt so important to me.

Totteridge – 45, Ventnor Drive

 We moved to Totteridge after just a few months and the decorating had to begin in earnest because every room needed attention. The house was described as having 'partial central heating' – this consisted of a single radiator in the hall! In Germany our house had been built with full central heating in the 1930s. Both of our parents had their house decorated in a very traditional manner and we wanted to be 'modern'. I shudder when I think of it now, but in the sixties these things seemed a great idea. Orange coloured feature wall in the dining room, flush doors, using hardboard panels and various pastel colours in bathroom and toilet. I suppose one has to go through such periods of rebellion in order to come round to a different way of thinking again much later.

in 2011

1961, 1964, 1966

Nils arrived on March 26th, just a few hours after Oscar's 40th birthday had ended. He was born in the examination room of Barnet General Hospital because the delivery rooms were already overcrowded. In those days one had to stay for 10 days in hospital after the birth of the first child, later ones would then be home confinements, if all had gone smoothly the first time. This is such a different way of thinking, compared with practices today when mothers usually only stay in hospital for about twenty four hours. Anyway, this delay gave my mother the opportunity to make arrangements for my father (aged 82) to be looked after and come over to help.

We had decided to bring Nils up bilingually and I would say that this worked well. During the day I spoke to him in German, in the evening and weekends it was English. He started nursery school when he was three but was just as fluent in English as the other children.

Nils was just over three years old when Michael arrived. By this time I had met another German woman, Brigitte from Tübingen, who was married to Michael Coffey. Our friendship was strengthened by the fact that their daughter Margaret was born just before Michael and two years later Monica beat Thomas to it by about a week.

Au Pairs

In these years several foreign friends had daughters, nieces or neighbours who wanted to come to England for the summer in order to improve their English. The first one of these was Elizabeth from France. She was seventeen and I was only twenty three and still pretty inexperienced, making it a learning adventure for both of us. Although we have not met many times over the years, we are still in touch today. The following year we had the daughter of a Swedish colleague of Oscar's, a very self assured young lady who told me exactly what I had to do! Then it was Cordula, a German girl who has also remained a friend. By this time I had become quite a little seamstress. Due to her help, the housework was always done pretty quickly and then the race was on for the sewing machine, because we were both running up cheap summer dresses. This was the time of the mini dresses and I doubt whether I would have shortened mine quite as drastically if she had not been around – after all I was now a mature (!) twenty six year old and Cordula just seventeen and daring.

Mr. and Mrs. Figgis

Opposite our house was the Manse where Mr. and Mrs. Figgis lived. Mr. Figgis was minister of the Congregational church around the corner. He was a truly exceptional man and I believe that he and his wife (a Quaker) were another important influence in my personal development. Houses did not change hands as frequently in those days as they do now and it was his habit to call on any house where a SOLD sign was displayed. He had called on the Coffeys and introduced Brigitte to me. He was a free thinker, politically involved and full of innovative ideas. One of these, rather too successful, was to start a club for Au Pairs on a Sunday evening. Many girls would have that evening off, but had nowhere to go. Only about a mile away was a monastery of the White Fathers where young men were prepared for the priesthood. They happened to have a few German and French trainees and Mr. Figgis persuaded the Fathers to let them come along to our Au Pair evenings. Unfortunately they became rather too enthusiastic and were stopped from coming for fear that they would discontinue their studies. – Mr. Figgis offered so much spiritually and intellectually, coupled with practical help that the congregation grew tremendously during his ministry in Totteridge. He persuaded me to join the church council as an 'Elder' – I think I was about half the age of the other elders. I have vague recollections of the meetings and some of the important decisions we had to make, but very useful for me were the Sundays when I had to help counting the collection. I could exchange some notes for a bagful of small change, thus keeping my children in dinner money for several weeks.

Just a Housewife

While the children were young, most of my friends stayed at home and looked after their children, returning to work once the youngest had started school. During the years in Totteridge I had a few attempts of broadening my horizons. First of all I joined an Anglo French Club that held its meetings at Barnet College. We had varied programs where improving the language was mixed with other cultural activities. Once Thomas had started nursery school I could think of a morning activity and joined a Current Affairs class, run by the WEA (Workers' Educational Association). Here I met Janine Tyler who had a son called Bernard at that time. The Tylers and Clemmetsens became lifelong friends. Bernard was joined by Colin and Richard and the four parents and six boys had many adventurous holidays over the years to come. Shortly before leaving London, I had read an article about professional women who were frustrated by having become 'just housewives' after having enjoyed various careers. They started "The Housewives' Register". I joined the local group, based in members' front rooms. We never had outside speakers, but took it in turn to prepare various topics for discussion. Soon after moving to Newcastle I heard of a local group here and joined it. These self-help groups provided valuable support for newcomers to the area and young mothers – some of the members I met in the seventies are still friends today.

Weekends and British Council Students

Our lives were similar to most of our friends and neighbours. The husbands went to work while the wives took care of the children and the house with a great routine of baking pies and cakes every weekend. Many Saturdays were spent decorating or gardening, but on Sundays, after church and lunch, we nearly always went out for a local walk, picnics and ball games with the boys.

Both Oscar and I had experienced living in another city or even country and knew that it is not always easy to get to know the local people. In 1961, when Nils was just 9 months old, we decided not to drive to Newcastle to celebrate Christmas with Oscar's parents, but to stay in London. Oscar contacted the British Council, an organisation always looking for people who would invite foreign students into their homes. Our first attempt was not quite the success we had dreamed of. It was a four-day holiday and a young Indian arrived on December 23rd. On Christmas Eve we took him for a drive and saw some logs for sale. We decided an open fire would make a lovely atmosphere and bought some of these logs. I think we were even greener than the logs! We put them into the fireplace, crumpled up some newspaper and the three of us took it in turn to blow and kindle this unwilling fire. Some time later we tried paraffin – how we did not blow ourselves up, I never know. About midnight, some of the thinner pieces had dried out sufficiently to catch fire – we were too exhausted to enjoy it by this time. All four days we could hardly get a word out of the young man and breathed a sigh of relief when at last we could take him home to his bed-sit. Imagine the scene: a freezing cold room with doors and wardrobes painted black and very little furniture. He invited us to sit on the edge of his bed and started to talk, and talk....and talk!

We invited British Council students for many years, but we had learnt our lesson – one night only to start with and if it went well, they stayed on and very often became regular visitors.

Taufiq and friend

There was a school's inspector from Sudan, a Tamil from Sri Lanka, and then those who remained friends for many years: Taufiq Lodhi from Pakistan who learnt cooking from his mother's letters and showed me how to prepare chicken Biryani; Josef Vellabonnici, a married man from Malta who attended a course in London and felt very lonely away from his family, and Fawzi Khattab from Syria who ended up in Malmö with Swedish nationality. We met Taufiq and Josef in London, the others later in Newcastle.

1962

22nd *November 1963*

At nights we stayed mostly at home with the children. One member of the Anglo French Club was reader in one of the London Newspapers and had arranged for club members to visit the paper. This was too tempting and we asked our neighbour's son to look after baby Nils. When we arrived in the big offices in Fleet Street we were told that we had to wait a little while due to some unforeseen events. The wait was not too long before we were allowed into the room where the ticker tape machines where whirring. Confusion and excitement in the room were mounting as the news appeared - letter, by agonisingly slow letter, that John F. Kennedy had been shot. What a day to visit a newspaper!

Timothy and Minnie Machinjili

Looking back, I don't know what possessed me to think about fostering when I already had 3 young children, one still in nappies. I imagine I had read about young mothers having suddenly to go into hospital with nobody to take care of the children left at home. I approached the Social Services and offered to help at such times. After some weeks they contacted us to say, that these situations rarely arose, because the youngsters were mostly looked after by family members, BUT they had a real need for longer term foster parents and that was the reason for agreeing to take in Timothy.

Timothy was a beautiful baby, 3 months old, who had been placed for adoption. Sadly it had been discovered that he would grow up severely disabled and the Social Services needed a temporary place for him until a permanent solution could be found. Could one say 'no' to such a request? However, it did not take long, before I really found the stress in the early morning and around teatime too much, because Oscar was never around at these times due to the long journey to the office. As mentioned above, I attended the Anglo French Club in Barnet and had noticed quite a few foreign students in the college. I approached the Principal and asked whether a young woman might be willing to come to live with us, free of charge, in return for an hour's help in the morning and about one and a half hours in the evening.

This is how Minnie entered our lives. She had a beautiful, warm smile, loved the children and quickly fitted into our household. She came from Malawi and had been educated in a catholic school until the ruler, Hastings Banda, ordered these children to be sent back to their villages. A few years later they must have had a shortage of professional young people and at the age of eighteen Minnie and her sister were ordered to study to become nurses, not locally, but in London. She was engaged to be married and deeply unhappy about these events. It took several weeks before she revealed all this to us, but gradually she grew calmer and more content now that she was part of a family again. We all benefited from this arrangement – I got help between 5pm and 7pm, really the only critical part of the day, while she had a family and received help with her studies. This is not how the Malawi High commission saw it! Somehow they must have been made aware of the situation and ordered Minnie to return to the B&B without delay. They said that they did not want their nationals to be exploited, but I am sure it was only to keep complete control of these young people.

It was not long after this drastic removal that I received a phone call from the local hospital "Are you the next of kin to Minnie Machinjili?" Our skin colours were on the extremes of light and dark, but clearly, she did not have anybody else to call on. The poor girl had tried to slash both her wrists and had ended up in the local mental hospital. Now I had to ask friends to look after the children, in order to visit Minnie. The first visit is something I will not forget. I had never been to a mental institution or a locked ward before. After being admitted to the ward I asked to be shown to Minnie's room, - the nurse just pointed to a woman sitting at a table, her face totally without expression and not at all recognisable as the bonny girl who had stayed with us. She answered my questions in a deep, husky voice and simply kept saying that she would soon die as she was drying out. Much later I read that some Africans are able to will their own death in this way. Luckily medication helped in the first instance and, once out of physical danger, Minnie went back, not only to Malawi but to her own village.

Rosemary

After that episode we had one more brush with fostering. By this time it was 1970, Nils was nearly nine, Michael six and Thomas four. Could we take in a twelve-year old girl for the last four years before she would leave the care of Social Services? We had not wanted to take in a child older than our eldest child, but the arguments were so convincing that we agreed to give it a try. Rosemary lived in a local authority home and came Friday night till Sunday night. She was well mannered, extremely bright and self-possessed. We had to be very careful not to let Nils feel that he lost his position as 'the eldest'. These were difficult months for us as well as the home, because Rosemary played off one against the other: "In the Home I never have to be in bed so early" and "At the Clemmetsens I am allowed to do…." We had just decided to end this situation and take her in completely when Oscar received the news of our move to Copenhagen. A short description of Rosemary's early years may explain her decision. Her mother's life had been chaotic; she would get to a point when she could no longer look after her little girl, gave it to the grandmother who then in turn passed her on to the Social Services. The cycle had been repeated many times. When we met Rosemary, she had formed a very good relationship with one of the carers in the home and confronted with the decision of leaving the home completely, she elected to stay, because this carer had been the first real anchor in her life. The lady tried to make Rosemary understand that she could be moved, but they left the final decision with the girl. I often wonder what may have become of her – did she follow in her mother's footsteps or did her undoubted intelligence and the guidance she received in the home, help her to stand successfully on her own feet?

1971 – 1972 Copenhagen

Schools

Oscar had been asked to work in Genoa for two years. I was so excited, immediately started to learn Italian and we investigated where the boys could go to school. This euphoria lasted about two months, when Lloyd's Register changed their plans and Genoa became Copenhagen. Although I had never been there, I knew it was another Hanseatic town, similar in appearance to Hamburg, cold and northerly – we were not too thrilled. Due to our previous investigations we knew that there was a German school in Copenhagen and we decided to enrol Nils and Michael there, even though we realised that some of the classes would be taught in Danish. Thomas was too young and went to the American school which was really an international school with English as the main language. Nils entered the third year and was sufficiently competent in German to be able to follow the classes that were taught in German and only had to struggle with the Danish. Seven was the intake year. Michael had already been to school for two years and found it hard to accept being in the youngest class again. But that was the least of his problems – he had the two languages to cope with. Oscar and I suffered the first traumatic months with him, often wondering at nights whether we were doing the right thing. And yet – giving up immediately did not seem a good option either. We persevered and before the first six months had passed, Michael was able to play with the children in the street, speaking Danish pretty fluently and much happier now.

Joys of Denmark

We lived in a small mid-terrace house, belonging to Lloyd's Register. Now we had far more time to spend together. Oscar's journey to work only took twenty minutes, and there was no decorating and very little gardening to do. We were determined to make the most of our stay in Denmark. We arrived in the summer and initially explored the local area. We lived in Virum, near the small town of Lyngby by Lyngby Lake. Almost opposite our house was the Freelands Museum, a collection of farm houses from many different parts of Denmark. This provided always a pleasant afternoon out. Not too far away either was 'Danish Switzerland' – not quite the Matterhorn, but an area of undulating woodland where the boys could run, cycle and make dens. Lyngby Lake became of interest in the winter when it froze over and – once the ice was thick enough – a tractor cleared wide lanes for skating. There was also an artificial ice rink we could use when the lake was not quite ready yet.

Car journeys took us north to wonderful beaches at Hornbaek and the Hamlet castle of Elsinore. From Helsingör it was only a short ferry trip to Swedish Helsingborg. There were castles and Viking ships to visit and a longer trip, involving 2 ferry crossings took us to Odense, Aarhus and Legoland. Foreign guests enjoyed the many sights of Copenhagen itself and visits to the Tuborg brewery. Rainy Saturdays, not too infrequent in the winter months, might see us visiting an IKEA store – long before that brand had invaded Britain. The main purpose of these trips was not shopping, but time for the boys to spend in the children's play area – a very new concept then.

Almost too many highlights you may think, but both Nils and Michael managed to injure themselves badly enough for hospital visits. Nils had to stay in for a few days and was admitted to a men's ward. Imagine my amazement when the tea trolley came round, offering tea, coffee and beer! Michael had to wait in casualty for so many hours that the profuse bleeding from his forehead had almost ceased by the time our turn came and we were able to take him straight home with us.

The Bach Family

While preparing for our stay in Denmark we remembered a distant relative of Oscar's: Maureen, who had married Danish Peter. Once safely installed, we contacted them, and found to our delight, that they lived not very far away. They also had three children, Lise, Andre and Anna. As Peter is completely fluent in English, they had decided to bring their children up bilingually. What relief to our boys to spend a Sunday, talking English to other children!

Festivals and Hygge

There are many lovely traditions in Denmark. In May, when the first little leaves appear on the abundant beech trees and the world changes from stark and grey to luscious and green, everyone comes out to party. Later there are maypole celebrations, bonfires and various national holidays. Christmas is an especially magic time and we all loved going to the town centres and larger shops, so beautifully decorated. Because it is often grey and wet, *Hygge* is an important concept. It translates as 'cosy' but involves so much more, particularly candles, pretty rooms, flowers, delicious food and – more candles.

A Night on the Tiles

Time for our return was coming nearer and it seemed a good idea for me to meet Mutti in Hamburg (about half-way between Copenhagen and Herzberg) for a few days. After locating my reserved seat on the train I found myself sitting with three gentlemen. I soon discovered that they were going to a shipping exhibition in Hamburg. Naturally I mentioned that my husband worked for Lloyd's Register of Shipping and as soon as they heard the name, they offered to look after me.

Although I did not know them, we had several acquaintances in common. Mutti was not due to arrive until the following morning and I decided that I could accept their suggestion of going to the Reeperbahn with the three of them that night. This is the notorious red light district in Hamburg, well-known to sailors worldwide, but for foreigners who just want to have a good night out with Bavarian Oompah music and beer, the Hofbräuhaus is a very safe and fun place to be.

A last Christmas

Oscar had to start in the Newcastle office in January 1973, but we had decided to spend a second Christmas in Denmark rather than in new and unfamiliar surroundings in Newcastle. Candles, red, green and white decorations, mulled wine as well as German and English festivities made this very special.

1973 – 1982 Newcastle

House hunting with Nils

In the November of 1972 Nils and I had been to Newcastle for a week to have a look at the housing situation and for him to sit the 11 plus examination. I was pretty determined actually to find a house we could move straight into when we arrived in January 1973, as a prolonged hotel stay did not appeal at all. At that time the housing market was very volatile and people were reluctant or financially unable to move and consequently there were not many houses on the market. We spent the days visiting estate agents and looking at a few houses. We stayed in the Imperial Hotel in Jesmond Road, which was rather in need of refurbishment at that time. The plumbing was terrible and I was kept awake at night by water noisily rushing through pipes in the wall, while I cried myself to sleep with worry about my responsibility. One of the houses we looked at was 64, The Grove, Gosforth. Access was difficult, as the Gas Company had dug up the road in front of the house. Entering the house for the first time, I was very impressed by the oak panelling in the downstairs hall. The agent then told me that the previous people he had taken there would not even go upstairs as the darkish hall had already put them off. This was lucky for us – because they had not seen how bright and attractive it was upstairs. I visited the local Lloyd's office to get advice regarding location and facilities in the area and was assured that Gosforth would be a good place to live in. How right they were.

The beginning was not very auspicious however. When we moved in a few weeks later, we had to bring everything in via the back garden – access from the front was still impossible. At that time we had no idea that a railway station was only a few minutes walk away. A good train connection to the city centre was an unexpected bonus, although the joy did not last long as by 1974 the service was discontinued and construction for the new METRO system began – this finally opened in 1980 and continues to this day to provide us with a superb transport link.

Nearly every day Nils and I passed the Civic Centre and we had noticed that immediately opposite was a theatre, called The University Theatre – now known as Northern Stage. That week they were playing Bert Brecht's *Three Penny Opera* and we decided to go – a bit of light relief from the house hunting. A completely new concept for me was the little bistro operation where small meals could be bought, quite exciting to us. This one evening made a deep impression on me for a variety of reasons and the theatre has remained a firm favourite over the years.

Leaving Denmark

On January 3rd, my birthday, we embarked once more on the journey right across Denmark, enjoyed the two ferry crossings for a last time before arriving in Esbjerg, on the west coast. We had time to spare before the ferry to Newcastle was due to leave and the boys asked to go to the beach. It was a glorious day with clear blue sky, hardly anyone on the white beach and Nils even braved the freezing water for a quick dip.

Lagganlia

Just weeks after we arrived, we saw a tiny advert in a national paper, inviting families to stay near Edinburgh during the Festival period. The children would be looked after and entertained while the parents were free to attend Festival events. The scheme was organised by Charlie Jackson, a family man himself with access to local college accommodation and students who would organise the children's activities. It was a completely new world for Oscar and me, never having been parted from the children, but more importantly, it led to life changing adventure holidays in Scotland. After running the Festival Family Holidays for a few years, Charlie invited families who had enjoyed these, to spend a week at Lagganlia, an Outdoor Adventure Centre, owned by Edinburgh Education Association. These were amazing weeks – every year the staff organised more challenging tasks for us. For me it was the first opportunity for difficult outdoor activities. Some years we got wet every single day. If it was not raining, we went canoeing and had to turn the boat over, or we went 'gorge walking' which involved walking up a mountain stream IN the water, wearing safety helmets. Oscar could not see the point of this at all and walked up beside the stream, thus keeping his boots nice and dry. We slept under the Shelter Stone high up in the Cairngorms and walked the Lairig Ghru, a pass through the Cairngorm range, linking Speyside and Deeside. We slept in a deserted barn, cooked on an open fire, and stirred midges into the food which gave us a good feeling of revenge after having been pestered by these mini-beasts so severely. The Tylers joined us several times on these trips, as did the children of a German school friend.

Further Education

Soon after we arrived in Newcastle I started to help in the Primary School attended by Michael and Thomas. Mothers used to go in one or two mornings a week and listened to the children reading or helped with other tasks. After only a few months the policy changed and untrained people could no longer be used in this way. I had toyed with the idea of becoming a teacher in the past (my mother had been a teacher) and decided now to enrol on a teacher training course. There were no college places left that year and it was suggested to me that I should enrol in an O-level class at Newcastle College. At first I felt this was a bit of a backward step, but it turned out to be a very good decision. I was 35 years old and had not written an essay since leaving school – even to produce 500 words seemed quite a daunting task at first. Now I had a full academic year to apply for a B.Ed. degree course and enrolled with Newcastle University. At that time the Education Department used buildings in Ponteland (they now belong to Northumbria Police). We had four days of tuition and a Wednesday off so that the young students could pursue sporting and other non-academic activities. I used these to shop, cook and clean the house as well as catch up with the enormous amount of reading.

We had a VW Dormobile and I used to sit with my books outside a sports hall while Michael had his karate lessons or in woodland car parks where the boys could roam and play with their friends. These were three very hard years and I had let it be known at college that I would not apply for a teaching position immediately. To my great surprise I was then offered a post as German Assistant at the college for a year. I remember this as a really enjoyable year. There was even time enough to co-write a book on essay writing in German "Der Deutsche Aufsatz". Obviously royalties have dwindled, but even in 2010 I still received a small amount from this little book.

A year later I started to teach German and English at Monkseaton High School. Now I was confronted with the reality of children. Some of them were eager to learn and progress, whereas others needed a great deal of patience and persuasion. I found the first year quite demanding, but from the second year onwards there were many classes and pupils I really enjoyed teaching. One highlight at this point: just a few years ago I met again, quite by chance, a boy who had always tried very hard, but did not find German easy. Subsequently he had gone to work in Germany, returned home, was now father of a boy himself and tried to bring him up bilingually.

Lloyd's Register and launches

Oscar had spent most of his working life on Plan Approval. However, LR had other plans for the last years of his working life and asked him to run the Newcastle Office. He had been away from Tyneside since leaving university and as a family we looked forward to coming to live in the North East. It was a new role for Oscar, which involved far more meetings away from the office and many other representational tasks. When we lived in London, the annual Staff Dinner/Dance was our only formal event. In Denmark we were occasionally invited to dinners and launch parties and I had already made myself one or two long dresses.

There was still a lot of shipbuilding on Tyneside in the seventies on both sides of the river. Between 1973 and Oscar's retirement in 1984 we attended more than one hundred launches. One very memorable one was a small vessel, launched sideways at Wallsend Slipway. The splash was huge and I almost thought the little boat would not right itself – of course it did. On the other end of the scale were several VLCCs (very large cargo carriers) and some of these were launched by royalty or other 'celebrities'.

A personal highlight came in 1977 when I was asked to name the 'Nessbank'. This ship had been built in dry-dock and was almost completely fitted out by the time I had to throw the champagne bottle at it. This was a great honour, really meant for Oscar, but obviously enjoyed by both of us.

By the time Oscar neared retirement shipbuilding had started to decline and Oscar became very active in the North East Coast Institution of Engineers and Shipbuilders. Most of the people involved in this had a shipbuilding background and tried to keep the industry going. Sadly, it was not possible for them to halt the gradual decline and closing of most of the yards. In 2010 Wallsend Shipyard sold their enormous cranes that had been a feature of the skyline for so many years. They were dismantled and shipped to India.

1976 – South Africa

In 1975 we had met a family from South Africa who had rented a house in the street behind ours. They had five children, the oldest of these being Ryno who was in the same class as Nils. After we had met them, we occasionally arranged to go out into the countryside together at weekends. On one of these trips they invited us to come and stay with them as we all enjoyed being outdoors and had many other interests in common. By going the following spring, before Michael was twelve, we only had to pay half fare for Michael and Thomas. It was a good saving and for me it was going to be an opportunity to meet distant relatives as well as visit the little town where Vati had stayed eighty years earlier.

We had not been out of Europe before and coming to South Africa while the Apartheid system was still in operation, was a great shock. Public buildings had separate entrances for

Whites and Blacks and if black people were seen in a white neighbourhood, they were servants. On arrival we stayed in Johannesburg for a few days, visited our relatives (Vati's nephew and his wife) and did some sightseeing. Then we hired a VW minibus, similar to the one we had at home and drove off towards the Krüger National Park where we were going to meet the Verster family. Along the roadside fruit sellers could often be seen. We stopped and bought a box full of oranges and another one with avocado pears. These were almost unknown in the UK and considered a great luxury. I decided to buy them for the experience. At lunchtime I tackled the first one of these 'pears', divided it up among us all and had to agree with the children that it was hard and tasted a bit like soap. After we had joined the Versters I told Charmien of my silly purchase. She took one look at the box, confirmed that they were rock hard and as yet completely unripe. A few days later that situation changed and a few of us became avocado addicts, eating the now delicious fruits on a daily basis.

One memorable day in the Krüger National Park was spent in a coach. The driver had a record with animal calls which he played after stopping the coach near a spot where lions had been seen. Sitting high up in the bus we watched a pride of lions sunning themselves contentedly after a large meal. The rarest of our sightings was the fleeting glimpse of a cheetah. We saw so many different animals and all of them impressed in different ways: the monkeys leap from branch to branch, shrieking with excitement, secretary birds strut importantly along the road, quite undisturbed by cars; giraffes and elephants in the wild are so stately and huge, hyenas look ugly to us, but are fascinating to watch when they hunt in large groups.

A night sleeping out under a huge rock overhang, high up in the Drakensberg mountains was an experience I will never forget. There were four adults and eight children so we needed food, sleeping bags and candles. This was our introduction to 'Verster's Stew' – we copied this idea many times in years to come. Recipe: take one tin per person and select a variety of items that can be warmed up together, for instance vegetable soup, corned beef, pasta in tomato sauce – your imagination and taste decide. The twelve of us wended our way upwards, carrying our goodies and a bottle of wine for the adults. By the time we reached our destination it was almost dark and candles had to be put right along the overhang so that we could see enough to feed the children and get everybody settled.

Nils jumped across a stream flowing along beside the narrow ledge and found a soft dry place. I joined him on this and indeed – found a better resting place than the sandstone shelf. When we woke in the morning we discovered that our mattress had been a large area of rabbit droppings. There had been no odour as they were completely dry and we all had a good laugh.

Active Boys

Bringing up boys in an urban area presents challenges and causes heart stopping moments to the parents. Michael was perhaps the most challenging of our three. He had found a kindred spirit in Nigel who lived two houses away. They invented exciting games: shooting flaming arrows from our to Nigel's garden. Unfortunately most of them landed in our neighbour's garden and they were not amused. '*Around the world in eighty days'* involved getting round our house without touching the ground by climbing from windowsills to drainpipes and anything else that would support their weight.

When Michael was twelve the first skateboards appeared. He and Nigel soon had a Saturday job, demonstrating skateboards in an outdoor shop in town. After a while Oscar was persuaded to construct a skateboard ramp that would be placed in our drive. The boys stood on the opposite pavements, looked both ways and set off, skating across the road. I could hear the loud Vroom as they soared up the ramp, followed by a different sounding Vroom when the board ran backwards – and back out into the road. Obviously without having looked both ways first! Later we bought a unicycle which all of them enjoyed - it was a much safer proposition.

Occasionally they camped in the garden, but the most exciting project was an igloo. One very cold winter the snow had the right consistency to cut blocks and Nils built a fine looking igloo. Unfortunately it was not quite large enough to accommodate his long legs. A lower 'lean-to' solved this problem and they all were able to spend a night in it, one at a time, before the thaw set in.

Survival Training

In the summer of 1982 I saw an article about a survival course, organised by the Local Education Authority (LEA). They had secured the services of survival expert and paratrooper Eddie McGee, who would teach basic survival skills over a weekend to be held on the Otterburn Moors. I made enquiries who would be eligible for this course and was told that anyone could go. I enrolled myself, Thomas and two of his friends. When I received a phone call from our local paper, *The Evening Chronicle*, a few days before the event, alarm bells should have sounded. However, the reporter explained that the reason for the special interest was the fact that Eddie McGee had just been involved in tracking down a multiple murderer on the North Yorkshire Moors who, following instructions from Eddie's book, was living rough. Obviously the LEA could use this publicity to secure funding for future courses.

The next event was a briefing meeting the day before we were due to leave. As our little group arrived at the venue, I immediately saw my problem. I was the only woman and at least ten years older then the few social workers on the course. Most of the boys looked like the proverbial hard lads and it was obvious that I had to rise to all challenges and not weaken.

Over the course of the next few days we learnt to build a simple shelter, make a hammock, kindle a fire, cook a skinned rabbit in the embers – first covering it in mud from the local stream which we had to pat around it – and were shown wild herbs and plants that could be used to flavour foods. Luckily we never needed these skills later, but the experience was well worth it and left lasting memories.

Friendship Force - The concept

In 1977 President Jimmy Carter was en route for London to attend meetings, but had asked to stop off in Newcastle because he wished to visit Washington Old Hall. The City Fathers did not want this opportunity to go by and organised a lunch for the president and anybody who was anybody and happened to be in town that day. To name just two – there was Mohammed Ali and also the mayor of our twin city of Gelsenkirchen. Over lunch it was mentioned that politicians and students were able to travel abroad fairly easily whereas ordinary people did not often have the opportunity to get to know people of other cultures better. The concept of home hosting was formed and some of the Councillors present had the organisational talents and influence to set up the first exchange. The first few of these exchanges were between Newcastle and Atlanta/Georgia. A Jumbo jet arrived from Atlanta, 250 Americans disembarked, 250 Geordies were excitedly waiting in the departure lounge and filled the plane for the return journey. Among the guests were TV announcers, traffic policemen, folk dance groups, classes of school children as well as many adults.

We were so impressed with the programme that we applied to join the following year. For our first exchange two girls were allocated to us; they were in their final year at school. It was a learning experience for us all and caused much laughter: they had never been abroad, were amazed at our tiny cars (I drove a Mini), the narrow streets and the ancient castles. I had never spoken to an American before. The following year we asked if we could host a couple. The Friendship Force motto is "Faces not Places". In the early years this meant that one did not know where guests were coming from or where the destination for the outward trip might be. I clearly remember sitting in the banqueting hall of the Civic Centre when the destination was going to be revealed. After much teasing "you won't find polar bears there" and "no point bringing beach wear" we were told that Newcastle was going to exchange with Las Vegas. Our early misgivings were soon put to rest, when we found out that our guests were not a dancer and a croupier, but a Spanish teacher and a mathematician who worked on the Nevada nuclear test site. We had a wonderful time with Bob and Daisy, because not only did we have similar jobs but also shared an interest in fossils and minerals.

In the early days hosting was only provided for a week and guests then made their own travel arrangements for a further week. Bob and Daisy intended to go to London and we repeatedly told them that they would have to book a hotel as it was June and a busy time in the travel industry. By the time the week was nearly over, they still had not made a reservation and gave the impression that they would really like to stay with us for another week. It had been half-term week and I had prepared nearly most of the food in advance. Now I had to go back to school and had no further special meals to offer. I think this shows what a wonderful concept the Friendship Force is. Bob and Daisy took day trips to Edinburgh and York while we were at work and just joined in our normal evening meals. Bob and taught us to play Black Jack, although we never played for money, and most evenings concluded with a merry round of this game.

Friendship Force – Special Moments

Over the years we hosted more than forty times, took part in about ten exchanges as 'Ambassadors' and went to visit and hosted FF friends on a private basis. Being part of this organisation has widened my horizon and established a firm belief in the Friendship Force Motto "You can make a Difference!"

Initially we did not think that we would be able to afford travelling ourselves. In 1979, when Nils was in his final year at school, we asked whether Nils and Michael would be able to join on their own. They were very fortunate. The exchange that year was to Raleigh/North Carolina. The Governor was keen to promote the programme and invited the boys to stay at Government Mansion while his wife and youngest daughter were over here, staying with the Lord Mayor. Nils was invited to spend a day with the governor, sitting in on all meetings and watch the various tasks involved. Michael was entertained by Rachel, just about his own age. At the weekend a helicopter took them to the family's home in the mountains, all experiences well out of the ordinary.

Here in Newcastle I thought it would be nice at least to meet the Governor's wife and daughter. A visit for morning coffee at our house was duly organised for them. When the guests arrived, there was one man more than I had expected. Over coffee he mentioned that he was working for the traffic police. Hours later it dawned on me, that this was the Security Man for the governor's wife and daughter. A year later a return visit was arranged and daughter Rachel was coming to stay with us, along with a woman in her thirties. A little wiser than before, I thought she must be 'the security', but was greatly relieved when I found out that they could share a room. I don't know what we would have done otherwise as my mother was also staying at that time and space was at a premium.

Hosting so many times was always a good opportunity for us to go out and visit the many wonderful places we have in the area. However, sometimes the visitors drew our attention to local things we did not know about. When Rachel and her minder/friend Pat were with us, Michael wanted to take Rachel to a now demolished shopping mall in town -The Handyside Arcade. This was of interest to teenagers but I had rarely been there. After a few minutes in the arcade, Pat wanted us to leave immediately. She then explained to me that several of the young men who were hanging round the shops were smoking dope. I would never have recognised the smell.

That same year we hosted Bill and his fourteen year old daughter Gail. Bill was pianist in a jazz band and they had arranged to play in several venues during the week of their stay here. Of course we had to do the chauffeuring and thus got to know some of the 'hot spots' in town. One of these venues was "The Mitre", formerly the bishop's house in Benwell. The beautiful stained glass chapel was now the performance room. It only lasted as a pub for a few years, but was used afterwards for several years as film-set for the children's TV series 'Byker Grove'.

In 1984 I was asked to be in charge of an exchange to Germany. Oscar and I talked this over and agreed to give it a try. Unfortunately plans changed fairly quickly and Germany became Bergen/Norway. The question was – would I still lead the exchange? Danish is very similar to Norwegian, so at least

I had a little knowledge of the language, also it would be an opportunity to meet Oscar's relatives in Bergen – and we agreed, not really aware of the implications. My baptism of fire came almost immediately. A Friendship Force members' meeting was held in the banqueting hall of our Civic Centre (we had about 700 members at that time). This was many months before the proposed Norwegian exchange and I had very little information to hand. Suddenly, quite out of the blue, I was invited to come to the podium and publicise the exchange. If the floor had opened up I would have been quite pleased to disappear. It did not and I had to stand up, tell the audience the few facts I already knew and make the exchange sound interesting enough for people to apply. It was a good initiation, because during the two-way exchange there were quite a few speeches to make, both in English and halting Norwegian.

In 1987 the Friendship Force celebrated their tenth anniversary. President Carter returned and about 300 FF members from around the globe flew in and needed to be hosted for a week of celebration. During the past ten years many countries had joined and we agreed to host three Korean ladies. They hardly spoke any English, but I remember much laughter and feelings of friendship. It also made me aware of cultural differences again. We had given them one small bedroom with a single bed and another room with twin beds. After some days I became aware that the small room was never used. These were three married women with teenage children who had not known each other very well before coming to us and yet they must have somehow managed to sleep in the two beds. At least they shared our meals and joined in all the activities we had planned for them. Other hosts were not so lucky. One family with Korean visitors discovered to their consternation that the guests would never eat with them, but retreated to the bedroom and prepared their own food in an electric wok they had brought with them. By contrast our ladies offered to cook a meal for us. The principal part was a large pan of very sticky rice, accompanied by various vegetables. After we had eaten this, came the surprising part. I had already wondered how we would ever clean the rice pan, when they filled it with water and put it back on the hob. After a while the rice had come away from the pan, they asked for soup bowls and ladled this unflavoured, watery rice out for everyone. The Koreans are very fond of Kimchi, a very fiery sauce. They had brought jars of this over, spiced the tasteless rice soup with this and sat in complete rapture while we tried to eat at least a small part of it.

The concept of staying with people works so well and we have always been lucky with our ambassadors. Some contacts were short-lived, while others became very strong friendships and have lasted for many years. We have often found that we shared more of our thoughts and feelings with these visitors than with local friends, where one tends to be more cautious when discussing personal matters. After the Korean experience we hosted and subsequently visited people from Japan, Brazil, New Zealand as well as Germany and Norway. Over the years travel has changed very much. Many young people have been on a gap year, have 'seen it all' and do not feel the need to join such a programme. Many distant places have become popular tourist destinations and yet – a tourist always stays on the outside, looking in, whereas a Friendship Force ambassadors is actually sitting INSIDE, participating in family life.

Tea Ceremony in a private house in Tokyo

1979 – Hundredth Birthday

Vati's 90th birthday had been a special event with a visit from the local mayor and many flowers. Ten years later he had  suffered a mild stroke and was bed-ridden, but still clear in his mind. In earlier years he had been fascinated by the number 88 and hoped to reach this age. After that birthday he said in his quiet way "I might as well carry on till ninety now" and having achieved this goal, he set his sights on the Hundred. He often asked how many weeks to go before July 18th. Luckily he was able to enjoy the day, the official visits, the many flowers and most of the grandchildren round him. It was only about this time that I realised how much I had missed by not questioning Vati to tell

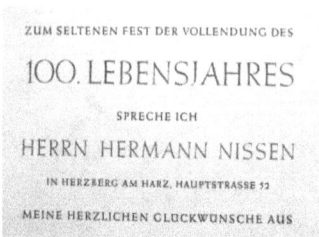

me more about his early years. He often asked me about life in the seventies – I told him about electric washing machines, the wider use of cars and planes and began to realise that these things had not even existed in 1879. Cars and planes have made the world a smaller place, television and the internet have brought the world into our living rooms.

1982 - Mutti comes to live with us

Vati died six months after his hundredth birthday and Mutti was alone. When she was nearly eighty we became increasingly aware that she could no longer live on her own in Germany. We asked her repeatedly to stay with us. She did not want to come while I was teaching because she hated being on her own in the house all day long. We felt it would be better if I gave up teaching for the time being, but I decided I would look for a part time teaching post. When I saw an advertisement for a "Homework Organiser" I thought I had found something suitable. To my surprise I discovered during the interview that it was not children's homework I had to organise, but act as a link for housebound ladies who wanted to knit, crochet or learn new handicrafts. They were members of Arthritis Care and I had to visit them in their homes. The interviewer, Mr. Henderson, had a very persuasive nature and eventually I agreed to give it a try. The work was voluntary, but I was reimbursed for expenses. In the beginning I found this aspect quite difficult to deal with. When I met new people who enquired what I was doing, a typical reaction was an immediate loss of interest as soon as they heard the term 'voluntary'. This problem disappeared once I realised how much people appreciated the visits and the fact that I could spend time with them and listen to their problems.

Bella

Mutti was nervous about staying in the house on her own, which had to happen occasionally. After giving the matter some thought it was decided that a housetrained, good tempered dog would be the answer. A visit to the Cat and Dog Shelter was arranged and we returned with Bella who proved to be a wonderful companion over the next 14 years. Unfortunately her pleasant temperament made her unsuitable as a guard dog, but luckily Mutti enjoyed her company and was more than happy to be left alone with her.

1983 -2002 Events

Foster Daughters

In 1985 we had become very friendly with the Jacobsens, a German family from Lübeck. They had brought their younger daughter Heike with them. She attended a local school while Dieter was working in Blyth. Unfortunately he had to return to Germany a year before Heike could take her A-levels. It was a difficult decision, but in the end they felt, it would be better for Heike to complete the course here before returning to Germany in time for university. For the first time we had a daughter in the house, which was very nice, especially as Nils and Michael had left home by then and we had got to know Heike well already.

Two years later, a school friend from Hamburg asked whether we could keep her niece for six months while she attended a local grammar school in order to improve her English. This time I was more apprehensive, because we did not know much about Maike. Anyway, we agreed with the proviso that she would have to leave if she did not fit into the family or caused too many problems. Like Heike, Maike was a very practical, sporty girl and gave us no problems whatsoever. She was seventeen, but very mature for her age and we managed to get her into the university netball team as well as a local tennis club. Apart from that she was only too happy to join anything we were involved in: walking group, outings to local places of interest and Friendship Force activities. The six months of her stay were enriching for us all.

In 1989 the Berlin Wall came down and after that many people from East Germany wanted to come to England. The minister of the German church was approached by Gudi (twenty eight), a trained nurse, who wanted to work in an old people's home. Due to my work with Arthritis Care I knew many of these and was able to give her some introductions. We offered to keep her for the first week or so. Gudi was charming. We enjoyed her company and soon offered to keep her for the six months she was going to work in Newcastle. She had very little English because they had only learnt Russian at school, but this soon improved and she was able to work with the status of a qualified nurse. Because she was trying to learn English rather than Geordie we frequently had to revise the pronunciation of her newly acquired vocabulary, explaining for instance that the dessert was not really called "pud'n".

A year later we visited Gudi in her flat in Leipzig. So soon after reunification houses and flats were still in a completely dilapidated condition, caused by forty years of neglect. Gudi's apartment had three large rooms and a narrow kitchen. The toilet was located on the half-landing, mid-way between two floors and used by several apartments. In the kitchen was a sink and a washbasin, but a friend had already managed to install a simple shower next to the broom cupboard.

Gudi introduced us to Franziska, a younger girl, who also wanted to improve her English. She had at least some basic knowledge and was able to work in the nursing home where I took occupational therapy classes. She stayed just three months before returning to Germany to start a course in dentistry so that she could to join her father's practice later.

Many years passed, before a friend asked whether we could accommodate a Spanish young woman, aged thirty eight, who wanted to attend an English course for a few weeks. A few e-mails passed to and fro, an arrival date in mid-September was discussed and then the bomb fell when she phoned to say that she had booked the flights, returning on December 10th! Pilar was energy laden and as Spanish as the women in Almodovar's films. She smoked and seemed to live on fruit and vegetables. However, the early misgivings were quickly sorted out. She smoked only in her bedroom, next to the wide open window, dressed in her quilted outdoor coat. Oscar often helped with her studies and occasionally she treated us to a vivacious flamenco dance, dressed in tight jeans and heavy woollen socks with her body completely transformed from the first moment that the music started. It was quite easy to imagine the ravishing flamenco dress. It was through Pilar that we were introduced to Nathalie – more of our last foster daughter in a later chapter.

Computers

In 1980 while Bob and Daisy were staying with us, Bob suggested that he would go with Oscar to purchase a computer. At that time hardly any of our acquaintances possessed one of these newfangled machines. The choice was an Oric, a small machine that was not very powerful but rather difficult to operate. It really was just a glorified word processor. By 1988 we bought our first Amstrad. This could do rather more than the Oric, but without any tuition it was quite difficult to work out what the words 'document' and 'folder' meant. Saving and retrieving documents also took a while to master. We still were the only people who had a computer and soon found ourselves typing membership lists for anything we were members of. At that time the fields for the database could not be changed which meant that you had to study the address list and find the longest item for each column (name, street etc.) and set up the field accordingly. Woe betide if later someone with an even longer name joined – that simply could not be accommodated.

1996

Actors

Every so often a friend who lived nearby called in for a cup of coffee. Her visits were always full of interest because she loved to travel and had a great interest in the theatre. This in turn had led her to offer hospitality to actors or musicians who were performing in Newcastle. At the end of one such evening we said, rather cautiously: "if you ever have no space, but know the performer, we would not mind giving this a try". Barely a week passed when she rang up with a very urgent request – the actor in question was on her doorstep and somehow she had overbooked. Minutes later John Quayle arrived and impressed us with his polite and charming manner. He was at the Theatre Royal for a week and to our amazement was always back about half an hour after the curtain had come down, ready for a cup of hot chocolate. We could not have had a better introduction to hosting 'theatricals', because he really gave us an insight into the life of an actor.

For several years we hosted for the RSC (Royal Shakespeare Company) when they were in Newcastle for six weeks at a time. Some of the younger actors were hardly ever to be seen – they got up late and returned home long after we had retired to bed. Others were happy to share a little of our lives either in the morning or after the performance. We hosted a violinist from Scottish Opera for several years and he even agreed to play at a Nursing Home where I held weekly occupational therapy classes.

Up With People

When we had been in the Friendship Force a few years, they received a request from an American organisation called 'Up With People'. This was a project, initially set up to get young people in San Francisco off the streets by teaching them a song and dance routine and then take this performance round the country. After a few years the scope had widened, school leavers could apply and the group even visited Europe. It operated by sending four young people to the next city, a week before they were due to give their concert. These four had to find accommodation for the whole cast of about one hundred as well as publicising the event. Many Friendship Force members agreed to host the cast. We ended up having two young women for the week before as well.

Americans do not travel light – the upper landing was soon occupied by their large luggage until we helped them to organise things a little better. Before long, water was dripping into the hall downstairs – this was coming from the jeans they had hand-washed and draped over the oak banisters. By this time I saw red and explained to them a few minor housekeeping points, especially as we also had an actress from the RSC staying at the same time.

One of the girls was called Sue Ellen and had grown up in Dallas. When she phoned the local radio station to get publicity for their show they thought she was teasing them – Sue Ellen was one of the main characters from the TV series 'Dallas'. She was pretty and vivacious, but completely disorganised. By the time she came to us she had already lost her passport, left her purse on a bar counter in Dublin and lost her handbag with most her money by leaving it on the backseat of car which was then broken into. Late at night we were all designing posters for their concert, even the actress joined in after her performance. The house was pretty crowded but it rang with laughter.

Special Events

A few events deserve special mention. In 1987 Oscar and I had taken an American friend to a song recital at Wallington Hall. Sharon, our guest, was an accomplished pianist herself and by the end of the evening we had made a rough plan for a *Musical Evening* to be held in our house a few weeks later. Our invited guests were very surprised when they arrived and found all the chairs set out in rows in the lounge, facing the piano. I had asked a few friends who were able to play an instrument or sing whether they would help and thus the first of many of these musical events came to pass. We held them for over ten years – even though it was not always easy to find new or willing performers. Once Oscar asked a busker, who was playing his clarinet rather well outside Marks & Spencer's, whether he would come and play. Amazingly he would not contemplate coming into a private house – he explained that he would be too embarrassed to face the audience! Obviously to him the faces in Northumberland Street remained anonymous and did not feel threatening.

Are holding a

**Coffee Morning and Cake Sale
On Wednesday 22nd of July 1992**

From 10:30 to 12:30
At 64 The Grove (near South Gosforth Metro Station)

Please come and bring a friend

A year later we started another event that ran for fifteen years. Esther, a friend at the Martin Luther Church held a coffee morning every summer at her home in aid of the German church and the Ponteland Care village. This gave me the idea of trying something similar for the benefit of the church and Arthritis Care. Ladies from the church came to help, brought wonderful cakes and to our amazement over eighty people turned up - we took £390 to be divided between the two charities. Initially it was quite strange because guests did not really know what to expect – could the Germans understand English for instance was a question asked by worried Arthritis Care members. Early reservations were soon forgotten and the event became a really popular meeting place.

Ashington Mine

Ever since coming to live in the North East, I had hoped that one day I might be able to visit a mine, even though I knew that miners do not really like women to go underground. My chance came at a lecture where I met a mining engineer who was about to retire. He was only too happy to arrange a visit as long as we could organise a small group. It was not difficult to recruit a few likeminded friends and off we went to Ashington. Formerly there had been three mines, although by 1984 only one shaft was still operational and long distances had to be travelled under ground. The largest distance was covered by lying flat on the ribbons that, in the other direction, transported the coal away from the face. Then there was a walk which ended in front of some sacking. We were told that beyond was the coal face. I had not come all this way only to stop here. Down on hands and knees we went, crawled under the dangling sack and at last we could see the huge cutting machine that rasped the coal away from the seam. Although the miners had help from these big machines, they still had to work doubled up in damp, dark and noisy conditions, coming to the surface just as black as their grandfathers had done.

Today we can visit the Woodhorn Colliery Museum, the last one of the Ashington mines. It serves as a stark reminder of what life had been like for thousands of men in the area. We had been privileged enough to really experience the hardship close up.

Salamanca

For several years I had been going to Spanish classes, first of all holiday Spanish, progressing to an O-level class and finally to an A-level course at North Tyneside College. A year is not very long to prepare for this examination. Just as I was beginning to worry, I saw a poster in the college, advertising Spanish language classes in Salamanca. Oscar was very supportive and it was agreed that I should enrol for 2 weeks in the *Colegio Miguel de Unamuno*. It was very strange being a student again, essentially being on my own in strange surroundings. Obviously I am a late developer – taking my B.Ed. degree aged thirty nine and now preparing for another examination in my forties. Nearly all the other students in my class at college were American social workers who had to learn Spanish in order to cope with the many Mexican immigrants in California. These two weeks were quite magical for me. It was much colder in early March than I had expected, but the sky was always blue and storks could often be seen circling in the sky on their return journey from winter quarters in Africa. The college was in the heart of the old city and I had to cross the Plaza Mayor on the way there. Salamanca has one of the oldest universities in Europe and every day I visited different parts of this historic city. One weekend a bus had been organised to take us to Ciudad Rodrigo, near the border with Portugal. Not as famous as Pamplona, but they also have bulls running through the streets. Young men put their lives in serious danger, when they run just yards in front of the bulls, jumping over the barriers to join the onlookers at the very last minute. At this event the humans are vulnerable rather than the bulls.

Birthdays

January 3rd 1988 was my fiftieth birthday. It happened to be a Sunday, furthermore it would be one of our Walking Club days. I did not want to miss the walk, but also wanted to have a party at home. Bob Geldof had just raised awareness of the famine in Ethiopia with the Band Aid concert and our friends were not surprised to receive an invitation for a 'Soup and Dessert' fundraising event for this cause. I had made large pans of soup and various desserts, was able to enjoy the day in the hills and still had forty guests in the evening. Unbeknown to me Oscar had ordered a special birthday cake, making it a truly wonderful day.

Oscar's seventieth birthday was celebrated at home with a dinner party with Michael and Thomas acting as waiters. Nils was working in Papua New Guinea and could only be with us in thought. Five years later in 1996 a more memorable event was staged. Some months earlier we had been together with David and Janine Tyler when it suddenly occurred to us that several members of our families were going to have a birthday ending with a Five or a Zero. Eight people would celebrate a total of 180 years. Choosing a venue was not easy because we were far-flung by now: London, Newcastle, Boston/US and

Berlin. Eventually we settled on a hotel in Grantham where we stayed for the weekend, walked during the day and partied at night. Nils brought a colleague from the Berlin office with him – our future daughter-in-law Sarah.

Astrid   Andy   Christa   Oscar 80 + sister Ingrid

Another combination party seemed to be called for in 2001, when Oscar was eighty and Nils forty. Nils suggested holding this event in Central Square – where Ove Arup have their offices now. It was wonderful to see many local friends of all ages as well as relatives from far and wide.

Weddings and Grandchildren

Valentine's Day 1995 inspired Michael to propose to Diane. The date was set as April 28th. Ten weeks is not a long time to prepare for a wedding, but they only planned to have a very small register office wedding and a meal with the close family afterwards. A few days later they asked whether the minister in the German church might be prepared to marry them. Luckily he was free and glad to come - only now they wanted to invite more friends. Where, oh where do you find a wedding venue just weeks before the event in spring? Most hotels had taken wedding bookings one or two years earlier. A friend suggested the Tyne Rivercruise boats. And this is what happened. With just weeks to go everything was planned, the bride looked stunning and there was space enough on the boat to accommodate all their friends.

Nils returned from Berlin in 1996 and proposed to Sarah on Logan Pass, Continental Divide of the Rocky Mountains while on a cycling holiday in the States. They were both working in the Birmingham office of Ove Arup and decided to hold their wedding Berrow Court on March 15th 1997. This made life very easy for us – we only had to turn up on the day. March was an exceptionally warm months that year, making a drinks reception with musical entertainment on the lawn possible.

Diane and Michael

Nils and Sarah

1999 was going to be our fortieths wedding anniversary. Oscar did not plan to make anything of this, but wanted to wait another ten years until the Golden Wedding. Nils insisted on celebrating the Ruby wedding and promised that we would hold another party in 2009. What a good decision that proved to be. We had a wonderful day at Horton Grange Country House Hotel – the relatives began to enjoy these meetings. The first few years of our stay in Newcastle we had only met some of the more distant family members at funerals and Oscar and I always felt it would be good to meet each other on joyous occasions as well.

This chapter seems to contain highlights only – and there were more to come in the following eight years. In 1997 Diane and Michael welcomed Matthew into the world not long after Nils and Sarah's wedding. Oscar was excited to be grandfather at last. We did not have to wait too long for Louisa. Her arrival was more complicated for the parents as they had moved house a week before Christmas in 1999 only to discover that the gas central heating needed to be completely renewed. They were lucky and found someone who was able to do the work just after Christmas and by the time Louisa saw the light of day on the 29th December the house was warm again.

Nils and Sarah did not stay in Birmingham very long, but were both able to find positions in the Newcastle office just weeks after their wedding. Isak kept us waiting quite a while, but by July 2001 there were three at Bemersyde Drive, the house Nils and Sarah had bought in the meantime. Anna joined the family in April 2005, quite a challenge for Nils who still tried to cycle with all the family at the weekends.

2001 and 2002

July 2001, one fine morning we received a telephone call from a local hospital to ask whether I was next of kin to Laura, one of the ladies I was very involved with through Arthritis Care. Could I come immediately as she was very ill, I went over as quickly as I could – alas she had passed away minutes before my arrival. She had asked me previously whether I would act as her executor, which meant arranging the funeral and disposing of her possessions, because she had no relatives at all. While driving home I wondered how I could cope, because we had friends from Germany arriving that day for a week's visit. Sadness turned to joy as soon as I came home – Oscar was beaming all over because Nils had just told him that Sarah had given birth to Isak that very night! A truly emotional day!

The following two weeks passed like a dream – alternating between happiness at home and the tasks I knew I had to carry out. Luckily our German friends were wonderful. They came with me to Laura's flat to find documents and other information we needed for the funeral preparations and were with me when I discovered that Laura had no money in the bank, just unpaid bills. The funeral Directors felt so sorry for me and agreed to charge a very minimal amount for their services and yet have a dignified ceremony. - August was a beautiful month after the trauma of July and we could enjoy baby Isak as well as Matthew and Louisa, now already six and three years old.

Events on a global scale were to follow. Sarah had asked in the morning of September 11th whether she could bring Isak round in the afternoon. When she arrived she seemed very agitated and asked us to put the television on immediately. Normally we never watched TV in the afternoon, but Sarah had heard some strange news at home and wanted to find out what it was all about. Thus the three of us watched in tearful silence as the planes flew into the Twin Towers in New York. At first we thought we were watching a film before the enormity of events really sunk in. Ten years later I can still recall our feelings on that day.

Just a few months later in the spring of 2002 two unrelated events happened. They disturbed us deeply and necessitated many hospital visits for months to come. First we heard that our friend Esther, then eighty years old, had fainted while making a pot of tea. As she fell, she badly scalded both her legs. She was in the burns unit for many weeks. Not long after this Thomas' best friend Len collapsed with total septicaemia and was rushed into the intensive care ward next to the burns unit. His survival was almost a miracle, and needed many months in hospital.

Nils and Sarah had invited us to join them in a cottage on Skye that summer and we set off with a heavy heart, worried about our two friends so seriously ill. Nils and Sarah themselves had developed health problems which finally had been diagnosed as an MRSA infections. Boiling all their clothes separately eventually cleared the symptoms. But more trouble was to come. In July, almost a year old now, Isak became feverish and had to be rushed to hospital. At first it was thought that he had an allergic reaction and after several days of treating him for this, we noticed that his knee was warm and swollen. At last it became clear that the temperature was due to the infected knee rather than an allergy. An emergency operation was decided upon and on a very dark night Sarah, Isak and I were sent in a taxi for the short ride from the RVI to the General Hospital. This trip took place in a torrential rainstorm which had flooded one of the road junctions so badly that the taxi driver stopped for several minutes before venturing across. Nils and Sarah had an anxious wait that night because an anaesthetist qualified to treat such young children had to come, before they could start to operate. Once the infection was cleared, Isak could soon return home and enjoy the rest of the summer. His knee healed up completely.

2003 Oscar's last year

Thurso

No major holidays had been planned as this was going to be a year of visits to family and friends. Sarah's mother Doreen was in the process of buying a flat in Newcastle and would not be in Thurso much longer. Just before Easter Oscar and I travelled north to stay with Doreen. We wanted to get to know her and the area where she had lived for about fifty years. The trip was blessed with beautiful sunny weather and we were able to enjoy the dramatic coast line, John o' Groats and some prehistoric monuments.

Alicante

We were not home for long before flying south to Alicante, where we stayed with Pilar's mother, Pilar and Miguel joining us for the weekend. The most memorable day was the Saturday. We drove westwards into the mountains. First of all we stopped at a chocolate factory before continuing on to Alcoy. This is an industrial town, similar to our Yorkshire mill towns. The last weekend in April, however, is very special because the battles between Moors and Christians that had taken place during the 'Reconquest' in the Middle Ages, are being re-enacted. Pilar was unstoppable – she ensured that we had good places to watch the impressive Arab parade (complete with camels and many bands) and got us past the doorman into a restaurant, reserved for participants only. I am still hoping to return to Alcoy one day.

Nathalie

One evening in Alicante, the neighbours' daughter Nathalie came in to meet the English visitors. She was just making plans to work in Edinburgh for about three months during the summer. As she had to travel via Newcastle anyway, we invited her to stay with us for a few days before going on to Edinburgh. When she arrived in Newcastle she had not been able to find a job in Edinburgh, but succeeded very quickly in getting a position in the Jury's Inn here. Nathalie endeared herself to us immediately with her quiet charm and ready smile and we were only too happy for her to stay with us for the whole time. Most days she did not have to start work until mid-afternoon. I have such pleasant memories of the three of us having lunch together, making it that little bit more special and often enjoying it outside in the garden.

Glyndebourne

Oscar's nephew and his wife had asked whether we would like to go to Glyndebourne with them. Tickets for these opera performances are very difficult to get and going with Alan and Marianne made the trip all the more enjoyable. Contrary to some rumours, the performance takes place indoors in a beautiful, modern opera house. A day at Glyndebourne is so special because of the long intervals. Everyone sets up picnic tables in the grounds on arrival early in the afternoon and returns there during the interval. Marianne prepared a splendid supper, Alan provided the wines and all we had to do was to sit back and enjoy ourselves.

Dressed for Glyndebourne with Alan

Bristol and Bath

After our stay at 'The Danes' in Slindon/West Sussex, we travelled by train to Bristol – a city we did not really know. Oscar, of course, enjoyed the nautical and engineering aspects, especially Brunel's Clifton Suspension Bridge. From there it is easy to visit Bath. This city has so much to offer. The Romans left marks of their culture and we can still see their splendid spa facilities today. Jane Austen took the waters in Bath although most visitors today rather come to admire the Georgian architecture which hardly has an equal anywhere else in this country. Another, personal reason for this journey was to visit Bernard, the son of Tante Gerty and Onkel Wilhelm. Like Oscar he was born in 1921 and did not feel able to come to Newcastle anymore. Bernard and Oscar had first met in 1959, the year we got married.

Wentworth Grange

Due to my longstanding involvement with elderly people I had become convinced that it is a good idea to move into smaller premises while one is still capable of coping with such a move. After almost thirty years in our house, we felt very comfortable there and just could not find a flat we liked. That is until Oscar's friend George telephoned one night with some news. A few months earlier he had moved from a large house into a flat in Wentworth Grange, just along the road from our house. Oscar had visited him several times already and expressed an interest – should a vacancy ever occur. Now the time had come, a flat was for sale and we immediately looked at it and made an offer. Obviously we had to put our house on the market and as luck would have it, the first prospective buyers arrived together with Nathalie from Alicante. This meant that her first few weeks were regularly disturbed by more such visitors until we received an offer for the house. In the meantime we had begun to clear out our 'treasures' from loft and garage and were already feeling quite stressed when suddenly – the flat was withdrawn from the market and everything came to a halt. We knew we should carry on sorting things out, but decided we would leave that for the winter months after Nathalie had left. That turned out to be a very good decision.

Whitby and Staithes

Nathalie had seen a poster of Robin Hood's Bay and really wanted to go there. Oscar liked the American painter Winslow Homer who had joined an artists' colony in Staithes when he worked in the North East from 1881 to 1882. A weekend visit was decided upon. The sun did its best to Make Robin Hood's Bay look like the poster for Nathalie, but by the time we arrived at Staithes in the late afternoon a cold wind had sprung up and some of Homer's stormy seascapes came to mind. The following day we took the North Yorkshire Moors Railway from Goathland to Pickering. Some years earlier we had done the forty mile Lyke Wake Walk, crossing the moors from East to West and we remembered the many times when we had to descend into a deep valley and climb out with failing strength on the other side. That had been a hard challenge. Now we were sitting comfortably in the little train that puffed southwards along one of these valleys. This was very much an easier option.

Beamish

The Saturday before Nathalie was due to go home we took her as well as Mathew and Louisa to the Open Air Museum at Beamish. There is so much to see and do in Beamish, more than can be achieved in a day. A tram takes visitors past all the different areas. I always like to start with the drift mine because it tends to get crowded later in the day. A drift mine lacks the drama of the descent into a deep mine, but it gives an impression of the low ceilings and cramped conditions the miners faced. Other noteworthy places are the Manor House, Stephenson's Rocket, the town with its different houses and the farm. We ended up at the Victorian school and had great fun running along with the metal hoops and other toys that Oscar still remembered from his school days. After dropping the children off at their home, we ended the day in our favourite restaurant *The Taste of Persia*.

October 9th 2003

Oscar did not want to miss church the next day, because he had tools to donate for a Third World appeal. His proposal for the afternoon was a visit to the Laing Art Gallery with friends Joy and Leslie. The men had already been to the Winslow Homer exhibition there, but wanted Joy and me to see it too. I so clearly remember Oscar reading the description for every painting, drawing my attention to things he particularly liked. We finished this perfect afternoon with a cup of tea in the gallery. Once outside, Oscar felt unwell and barely made it back to the car. We rang 999 and the ambulance arrived within minutes. A heart attack was diagnosed and we ended up in the Royal Victoria Hospital. Oscar had been my best friend and companion for over forty years and it was a privilege to be able to stay by his side day and night for the few more days granted to him. As a family we were blessed – we knew that our husband and father had enjoyed life to the very last moment and every member of the family, including the three grandchildren had come to his bedside to say goodbye.

2004 Wentworth Grange

Moving and first visitors

Just days into the New Year we once more received an unexpected telephone call. The flat in Wentworth Grange had been put on the market again – were we still interested? Our circumstances had changed in the last six months, but friends  and family encouraged me to buy the flat, especially as Oscar had been involved in choosing it. The following four months convinced me that my earlier decision of moving at a convenient, planned time had been a good idea. For the first time I needed to make all my own decisions, sort out financial matters and now also had to buy and sell property as well as clearing our house out. I was ready to move, but the vendors did not leave the flat until mid-April. These three months felt long and difficult.

It took several weeks before electrical and decorating work had been completed and I had to leave to lead a Friendship Force exchange in Germany before the bathroom had been completed. Faith in the plumber was rewarded – everything was finished on my return.

Partners

Thomas felt that we were the partners now and that he had to take on more responsibilities. Sharing out the work was not too difficult, but problems arose when Daleks and Cybermen threatened to invade the living room. Luckily we came to an amicable agreement and banned these evil creatures to his room and the passage in order not to frighten future guests.

Several visitors stayed that first summer, no doubt curious where we had ended up. The most severe test came when the German Friendship Force group came to visit us in September. Most exchanges end with a nice dinner in a hotel or restaurant. We had booked a room in a pub about half an hour's drive from Newcastle. I had been in regular contact with the owner after we had booked the dinner for forty guests – imagine the shock when at 5.15pm on the day of the party I received a phone call from her, to say the cook had not turned up and the pub would not open. A few quick consultations with other committee members resulted in the decision to hold the party at our flat, based on a Chinese Takeaway meal. Our German guests were wonderful – in half an hour we had rearranged the furniture, sorted out eating utensils and made a shopping list. By 6pm the Takeaway opened, took the order to be delivered at 7.45 and we went off to the Supermarket to buy drinks and desserts. Although the flat is spacious – there was very little room to spare by the time the guests with their extra chairs had squeezed in. The food arrived on time, none of it ended up on our new carpets and everyone agreed that we had far more fun than the original plan would have been.

Holiday Highs and Lows

Extremes

Over the years we have had many very different types of holiday and I firmly believe that our lives have been enriched because we have rarely shied away from new experiences. Easter 1986 we decided to go hostelling in Galloway and chose a hostel with the motto: 'Come to Minnigaff and watch it rain'. It did not rain, but it certainly snowed. We arrived Good Friday afternoon at the old school building. It only had two classrooms - one used for the men's, the other for the ladies' dormitory. The hostel had been closed all winter and due to the extreme cold, the warden had allowed some people to place their mattresses round the kitchen range. Alas, there was no room for ours, but we were told we could use as many blankets as we liked. These were old, grey army blankets. I used seven of these, could hardly move under the weight, but shivered all night. On Saturday we set out on a walk in the snow. By mid-afternoon we found ourselves in a complete white-out – quite a scary experience. We lasted one more night and then decided to drive straight home on Easter Sunday.

Just a few weeks after Easter Oscar and I were booked on a tour to Egypt. The first two nights spent in the Cairo Sheraton on the banks of the Nile. I was amused by the rug in the lift with the welcoming words: 'Good Afternoon' woven into it. Would this not look a little silly in the morning? I need not have worried, four times a day these mats were changed to greet guests appropriately. One could hardly have had a greater contrast than these April holidays and yet – I would not have wanted to miss either.

Soviet Union

Some of our more extreme holiday adventures were inspired by Nils. As soon as he had graduated, he had embarked on a two year cycle trip round the world and had written every week to tell us about his adventures. We were too old for many of the experiences he had had, and yet – it made us more daring. I have already written about our trip to South Africa in 1976. In 1989 we made another very impressive journey, this time on the Trans Siberian Railway. It was still the Soviet Union and all travel arrangements had to be booked through Intourist. We had to be with the guide at all times and meeting ordinary Russians was not encouraged. There was sightseeing in St. Petersburg and Moskow and like most tourists we were impressed by the underground system and the palaces that had been restored to their former glory. The journey became special once we had boarded the seven-hour flight from Moskow to Khabarovsk, in the extreme east of the country. Vladivostock was a naval port and forbidden to foreigners. In the hotel in Khabarovsk we met Russians for the first time and were also free to wander around by ourselves. It was sad to see how few things were displayed in the shops and the poor quality of any available fruits and vegetables on the market stalls.

At Khabarovsk we boarded the train that was to be our home for the next four days. Two of us had to share a compartment. The Russians had six bunks in the same space, three on each side. Most of them kept the beds up all day, sleeping and reading until the train stopped. Many people got out at the stations: the tourists wanted to take photographs while the Russians bought their provisions. There were always old ladies, wrapped in many layers of clothes, selling hot boiled potatoes and sometimes nuts or pickles as well. Even when the train was running hours late, the steaming potatoes were waiting for the eager customers.

We had our meals in the dining car. The first day we each had a whole single ply paper napkin. On the second day it was a quarter square each and by the third day we only got a tiny triangle of paper. The food went in a similar way. The soup became more and more watery and one day it looked suspiciously as if the remnants from the previous meal had been tipped into it as well. The cook did a good trade selling food off to local people. At every station a queue formed by the dining car and waiting people handed their containers in to be filled. I am certain that their need was far greater than ours.

Every trip to the Soviet Union had to include an industrial town in Siberia. Although nobody in our group was looking forward to this – it turned out to be one of the most interesting parts of the journey. The hotel served alcoholic drinks instead of insipid lemonade, local people were using the same restaurant and were able to join us during the evening. For the first time we saw well dressed people in warm fur coats and our guide did a lot of shopping – she told us she could not get the same items in St. Petersburg. However, we did not see shops, selling the clothes we saw, but found out that the 'shops' were in unmarked flats in apartment blocks and veteran soldiers or other privileged groups knew where to find them.

Visits in Bratsk included a nursery school and the enormous hydroelectric dam which is the reason for the city being there in the first place. Wages in Siberia at that time were about twice as high as in Moscow, in order to persuade people to live and work in this inhospitable climate. We were there in November and the temperature was minus 15° C.

Historically and architecturally a more interesting city is Irkutsk near Lake Baikal. In the 19th century many artists, officers and nobles were sent there into exile and many of their wooden houses are standing today. Lake Baikal is a favourite place for newly weds and we were invited to join a celebration. The little party consisted of bride, groom and two friends. They had a bottle of sparkling wine and four plastic mugs and yet they were happy to share the little they had with us foreigners. It was a humbling experience. – I have often wondered what life is like now and yet I fear that nothing has changed very much for the ordinary people even though oligarchs are immensely wealthy.

Beware of the young men

Most travellers return from the Middle or Far East with tales of having been accosted by pushy young men wanting to sell all but the family silver. Let me tell you why I still give them the benefit of the doubt.

Our first really long distance trip was to Thailand in 1991 on the way back from seeing Nils in Papua New Guinea. We spent a few days in Bangkok and were standing on top of the Golden Temple when a young man approached us and asked whether he could practice his English with us – I found out later that this is a very popular trick to get people into a good mood. We were new to this and agreed to talk to him and in return he pointed out various landmarks to us. When we were about to leave, he asked whether we would be interested to attend a cultural show at the university that evening which was going to be put on by Thai History students. He told us where we had to meet him, but we were somewhat wary and consulted the tour guide back at our hotel. She suggested that we might as well take a chance as long as we left all valuables and passports behind and only took a small amount of money along.

Prepared for anything, we took a taxi (a real car rather than a *TukTuk*) and found the young man waiting for us. The building really was the university and the entrance fee was quite modest. He was most concerned for out wellbeing, especially for Oscar whom he treated with great reverence. Other foreigners were in the audience, mostly accompanied by business friends. We had a magical evening with delicious food, first class entertainment and the company of a local. At the end of the evening he declared that car taxis were far too expensive, hired a *TukTuk* for us and paid the driver on departure, the fare a fraction of what we had paid earlier.

A day in a remote town of Tunisia turned out rather differently. Barely arrived at the central mosque, a young man offered his services as a guide. We politely declined, told him we had a map and guidebook, but to no avail. After a while we relented and let him take us round the city. He must have spent well over an hour with us, taking us to places we would never have found on our own – and yet, we remained suspicious. Almost back at the mosque, he guided us towards a carpet shop. Aha! We thought this is it – and refused to enter. You should have seen the horror on his face – of course we did not have to buy a carpet, but the roof had the best view of the mosque. Mollified we followed him and had just decided that he was genuinely nice when the trap sprung: could we give him $10 because it was nearly graduation day and he wanted to stage a party for his friends. We did give him some money, but it left us a little disappointed.

Another day, another city. This time I was in Cairo with two women friends. Again we were outside a mosque, this time it was Al Azhar Mosque and university. Unfortunately it did not open to visitors for several hours. As we deliberated and wondered how we would find our way to the Blue Mosque instead, especially as we could not read the Arabic for *Acsunqhur* = Blue, the proverbial young man appeared. We had no intention to pay for a guide and tried repeatedly to get rid of him. He spoke fluent American English and told us that it was his day off from working in the local hospital as a pharmacist and he would be delighted to help us appreciate his city. At last we relented and another wonderful experience ensued. We might never have found the little mosque and once there, the aged keeper seemed very unwilling to let three European ladies in. Our new-found friend paved the way and no money changed hands apart from a donation for the poor box at the mosque. Let these three stories suffice to explain why I still fall into traps sometimes, because when the young men are genuine, an ordinary sightseeing day is suddenly greatly enhanced.

Holidays with Thomas

China had been a longstanding dream which became reality in 2007. It was a group holiday, but we had made our own travel arrangements and arrived several hours before the others. It was lunchtime and we were keen to venture out into the great unknown. The doorman at our hotel told us that across the square we would find a Pizza Express; however I could not see the point of eating American food in China. Luckily nearby we found a Chinese restaurant which looked inviting and was very busy with office workers out for their lunch break. We decided to give it a try. The menu was very extensive, but exclusively in Chinese. Luckily it was lavishly illustrated and we chose, what we thought, would be a bowl of noodles and a side salad. What actually arrived were white strips of cold, marinated seaweed and a pungent vegetable salad which even I could not manage to eat. Not a good experience.

Ten days later, at the end of the holiday we returned to Beijing and stayed in the same hotel. Our fellow travellers were too exhausted to leave the hotel, but Thomas and I decided to return to the restaurant across the square. Again we were the only foreigners, but this time we asked for help and managed to explain that we wanted to eat something hot. The waiter could not do enough for us, showed us dishes prepared for other diners to help us chose and generally made such a fuss of us that we ended up staying a long time. It was a memorable meal and proved the saying: when at first you don't succeed....try again!

Reflections

Grandchildren

Isak, Matthew, Louisa 2003

Matthew and Louisa   2009   Anna and Isak

Oscar and I had always hoped that eventually we would become grandparents and this wish was granted, although Oscar was no longer there to see Anna. Long forgotten childcare skills had to be remembered and weekly trips to Nursery school and later Primary school became a routine. Often we had a project on the go, painting, drawing and creating amazing things from cardboard tubes and boxes. I am so grateful to the children to have allowed me this second childhood. We played football down by our garages or on the fields nearby and built wigwams from sticks in Gosforth Park. An annual highlight is always the Christmas play, originally written by me, but responsibility gradually passed on to the children themselves. Usually the first and only rehearsal takes place at our flat on Christmas Eve, giving busy mums a few hours to do their final preparations. The grand performance is then staged either after church that night or following lunch on Christmas Day.

When my father was born, steam engines were already used to propel ships and trains. The motor car was in the process of being developed whereas the first flight did not take place until 1903, about the same time as the first radio transmissions were made. One hundred and thirty two years have passed and the world has become a completely different place. The invention of the microchip in 1959 speeded all these developments up enormously. We can watch events on the other side of the globe as they happen; video conferencing and Skype have made it possible to speak to people anywhere in the world and actually see them. My grandchildren use computers so confidently and live in a world that 'is connected' at all times and this inspired me to think back of my own childhood and that of my children. The speed of new developments is simply breathtaking. These pages may give them a little insight into the lives of the two previous generations.

My life has been guided by two phrases *"Always a little further"*, the title of a book Oscar gave me to read when we were first married, and *"I try anything once"*. Both of them have resulted in some anxious moments but far more often in added excitement and unexpected and wonderful experiences.